Psychology of Disorganised Personality

About the Authors

Maj. Gen (Dr.) Ranjit Singh, AVSM, VSM (Retd.) and Professor Emeritus was born on 5 June, 1953 and was commissioned into the Army Educational Corps of the Indian Army on 16 December, 1978 and retired from active service on 30 June, 2012. Prior to joining the coveted position as Vice Chancellor of Central University of Haryana on 22 August, 2013, he held the position of the **Vice Chancellor, The Global Open University, Nagaland** and has served as a **Nominated Educationist Member of the Navodaya Vidyalaya Samiti.** He is also holding the position of the President of NEHA Foundation, an NGO dedicated to enhancing women empowerment curbing foeticide, developing the personality of youth and welfare of retired defence personnel and martyrs.

Dr. (Mrs.) Rekha Sinha (b. 1958) is currently Professor of Psychology, T.M. Bhagalpur University, Bhagalpur. She has contributed more than 20 research papers to the reputed national and international journals of Psychology and other social-sciences. She has completed two UGC Major Research Projects and has also authored one book, entitled : Organised and Disorganised Personality : A Comparative Study. Organizational, Industrial & Environmental Psychology are the areas of her interest in research

Psychology of Disorganised Personality

Major Gen. (Dr.) Ranjit Singh
AVSM, VSM (Retd.), Prof. Emeritus
Vice-Chancellor, Central University of Haryana

&

Dr. (Mrs.) Rekha Sinha
Professor, University Department of Psychology
T.M. Bhagalpur University
Bhagalpur

CONCEPT PUBLISHING COMPANY PVT. LTD.
NEW DELHI-110059

ISBN-13: 978-93-5125-072-2

First Published 2014

Published and Printed by

Concept Publishing Company Pvt. Ltd.
Regd. Office:
A/15-16, Commercial Block, Mohan Garden,
New Delhi-110059 (INDIA)
Phones : 25351460, 25351794, *Fax* : 091-11-25357109
E-mail : publishing@conceptpub.com
Website: www.conceptpub.com

Editorial Office:
H-13, Bali Nagar, New Delhi-110 015, India.

Preface

The social disorganization perspective arose after World War I in response to a particular set of circumstances in both the larger society and the field of Sociology and Psychology. It is a clear presentation of the endless problems that face any country. No society is a perfect picture of social organization. Social problems arise in the matrix of personal and social disorganization and are clearly the consequences of the disruptive processes of society. Social problems have many ramifications and worldwide implications. Modern society is beset with innumerable difficulties, its problems are too complex and interrelated to be explained adequately from a single point of view. It is evident that rapid, far-reaching, and unequal changes in society accentuate social disorganization and produce the underlying conditions of the major social problems.

The growth of population has been very rapid and large. The living and working conditions of the individual have been most wretched. The living standard is probably lowest in the civilized world. Majority of the countrymen are ill-fed, ill-housed, ill-clothed, ill-educated, ill-doctored and ill-nurtured. Longevity of life is small and in spite of development in health programmes the country is even now the cesspool of endemic and epidemic diseases taking heavy toll of life each year. The streets, the bathing-ghats, the pilgrim centres, and bus stops all throng with multitude of beggars, mendicants and truants of all description, and the industrial, mining and plantation areas with that section of society known as the 'prostitutes' along with the vices of gambling and alcoholism. Millions are physically and mentally handicapped and are, therefore, a burden on society. Yet another millions are unemployed and underemployed, which are a further drain on the scanty resources. Early marriages are rather the rule and widow-remarriages an exception. The women folk are subject to social injustices at the hands of their men folk and the maltreatment that is meted out to what are known as Depressed castes and Criminal tribes is clearly visible. These and many more are the situations which demand an urgent attention of all concerned.

Moreover, in India there is a confusion of values and attitudes in different spheres of social life, which makes both personal and institutional adjustments very difficult. Industrialization is changing the whole pattern of relationships in the making of a living, but the caste and the joint family relationships and attitudes are not in accord with the demands of industrial living. Thus misfits, maladjustments and sufferings accompany anti-social attitudes and behaviour. A wise, social, economical and psychological planning, therefore, is needed which alone can prevent the problems and contribute towards the positive promotion of mass welfare in India.

The main aim of this research is to describe typical present day problems (Alcoholics, Beggars, Criminals and Prostitutes) in the setting of Indian society. In this study tools of empirical research were applied to differentiate socially disorganized groups (Alcoholics, Beggars, Criminals and Prostitutes) from normal people on the basis of personality variables. The book has four chapters in all. The first is introductory, the second deals with the sample, the tests used and the procedure of the study. Results and discussion thereof have been given in the third chapter. Chapter four provides the summary, limitations of the study and some suggestions for future researches.

Contents

I
Introduction

In a dynamic society, such as the modern social order, both the structure and the functions of groups are continuously changing. Whether slowly or rapidly, group life is disrupted by the processes of social opposition and disorganization.

Social problems are likely to arise when the balance and unity of society are upset. This condition may be occasioned by rapid and uneven social changes. Disorganization is fundamentally a process or a combination of the processes of social opposition and disintegration. A society experiences disorganization when its parts lose their integration and fail to function according to their implicit purposes. The general characteristic of disorganization is that the separate functions of the members of society are not being successfully performed. The decline of unity and harmony is a primary condition of disorganization. The general symptoms of disorganization in society include formalism, the decline of sacred elements, individuality of interests and tastes, emphasis on personal freedom and individual rights, hedonic behaviour, population heterogeneity, mutual distrust, and unrest phenomena. Deviations from conventional standards are examples of quasi disorganization which express themselves in many ways in contemporary Indian society.

Deviations from norms which are tolerated or which provoke only mild disapproval are obviously of little concern to a society. Only those situations, in which behaviour is in a disapproved direction, and of sufficient degree to exceed the tolerance limit of the community, constitute deviant behaviour. The behaviour which deviates from norm of the society is called deviant behaviour. This includes such deviations from norms as delinquency and crime, drug addictions, alcoholism, mental disorders, suicide, marital and family maladjustment, problems of old age, and discrimination against minority groups. Probably no two people can agree on the exact name of an adjusted or a normal person. Who is normal? Who is adjusted and has a balanced personality? In a quantitative term, a normal person would be one who possesses the attributes or qualities of the average, the mode, the usual or the majority, and abnormal person would be a deviant from the usual or average. He is not the ideal person or one with unusual qualities. But this does not indicate an evaluation of the characteristics of normal *versus* abnormal. So in one word one can say that normal person is one who adjusts himself in every aspect of his life. Personality adjustment implies a balance and integration of the various traits of personality and a fairly-successful orientation of the person to the social world.

Some writers refer to the existence of what has been described here as deviant behaviour as social disorganization and the society as being "disorganized". A state of disorganization is often thought of as one in which there is a breakdown of social controls over the behaviour of the individual and a decline in the unity of the group because former patterns of behaviour and social control no longer are effective.

Society is an organized collectivity of persons made up of a network of interconnected groups and organizations. We are born in organizations, educated by organizations and most of us spend much of our lives working for organizations. The individual has common needs and interests which account for the phenomenon of organization. Accordingly, we have organization patterns like the family and community on the one hand and the state, associations, clubs etc. on the other.

These different patterns of organizations perform the function of serving the fundamental societal needs connected with food, procreation, education of the young, protection of the individual and the group, communication, recreation, religion, care of the needy etc.

On the other hand, social disorganization represents the reverse of social organization. It occurs when there is a change in the equilibrium of forces, a breakdown of the structures, so that the former patterning no longer applies and the accepted forms of social control no longer function effectively.

Thus social disorganization is a process by which the relationship between the members of a group is broken or dissolved. Since group is the cluster of social relationship among its members, and social disorganization is literally the process of breaking down the group, we can also expect such disorganization in family, neighbourhood, community or nation. And ultimately all these will lead to disorganization in the individual's personality. Each individual member has got a large number of group ties but all of these are not broken at any one time. The individual may be disorganized in so far as some group pattern is concerned, but he may maintain his relationship with others. When these patterns are disturbed or broken either due to a change in equilibrium of forces or a breakdown in social structure because of the dissolution of institutional relationship, social disorganization is said to exist. So both social organization and disorganization are relative terms. The social process is the central core of human life. Social interaction and co-operative living are necessary for human existence. They are likewise essential for the development of personalities, group organization and culture, and the maintenance of the social order. A successful society achieves a relatively stable system of organization that is adopted to the physical environment and that enables the members to carry on the generally accepted tasks of the group without undue disruptions. Social problems arise in the matrix of parental and social disorganization and are chiefly the consequence of the disruptive process of society. These problems reveal an upward trend in their incidence. The process of disorganization includes conflicts) certain forms of competition and social differentiations, and similar processes of social opposition and disintegration.

According to Cooley (1909), social disorganization is due to urbanization and also the result of disintegration of traditions. Thomas and Znaniecki (1921) who developed "Social disorganization" as a sociological concept defined it as "decrease of the influence of the existing social rules of behaviour upon the individual members of the society." This approach seeks to explain a social problem in terms of the weakening social ties between an individual and his groups. The individual's inability to cope with the institutional frame of his group may create disorganization.

Ogburn (1922) observed that people accept new tools more readily than new ideas. According to him there are two types of culture, material culture and non-material culture. Material culture changes much faster than non-material culture. Stated another way, changes in customs and rules tend to lag behind those in technology, which is, as Ogburn said, "cultural lag". The principal source of social disorganization, in his view, is this uneven rate of cultural change. He further maintains that the different parts of culture are interdependent and when different parts change at different rates, one part can get out of phase with another and produce disorder.

As a system of classification and identification, the concept of social disorganization looks profitable. As an approach, it has its limitations in explaining the causation of all social problems. Fuller (1937), in his sociological approach, pointed out in a significant observation, that a young delinquent may be well adjusted within his gang. Therefore, he could only be considered a prey of social disorganisation in the context of the wider social whole. Mowrer (1942) considers disorganization as "the normal consequence of social change as well as the natural condition to social change." He also said that personal disorganization represents behaviour on the part of the individual which deviates from the culturally approved norm to such an extent as to arouse a social disapproval.

Kramer (1943) said that social disorganization refers to the failure and dissolution of the relationship between individuals, who are themselves inevitably involved in these processes. A disorganised society, therefore, is composed of individuals whose lives are more or less disorganized due to confusion of status and roles, contradiction, conflict and change in social values.

Individual disorganization and social disorganization operate in a vicious circle; the disorganized individual produces further disorganisation in so far as his behaviour affects others. The disorganized individual is unable to play his roles properly in relation to others and hence a chain reaction of social disorganization. Individual and social disorganization are largely different aspects of the same problem. Majority of the disorganized individuals are the product of the society of which they are the members when group consensus breaks down; due to social change, some individuals are rendered unable to play their roles in a manner acceptable to the society.

According to Faris (1948), who also seeks to develop it as a sociological concept, disorganization refers only to the failure of institutional mechanism—to the disorganization of bonds and controls, which make social team work, carry out its functions.

Durkheim (1950) has pointed out that social disorganization is the result of technological changes in the society. Technological development leads to division of labour and this division of labour gives birth to complexity, as a result of which social equilibrium is disrupted and social organization is disturbed. In this way, Durkheim defines "social disorganization" as a state of disequilibrium and a lack of social solidarity or consensus among the members of a society. To Lemert (1951) "social disorganization is a very general term meaning unbalance, disequilibrium, and extensive conflict between the groups and institutions of a society."

Thus, social disorganization is conceived of as a failure of social rules, norms, culture, social values etc., and its root cause is social change. Now let us examine briefly each of these concepts and see how changes in them lead to disorganization.

Social Norms

The social order that people share and maintain is at the same time a moral order. Social life is not possible without some agreement upon and relative adherence to moral rules and standards that define what people "ought" to do in given situations. Only a man alone in a desert is and might be free of moral restraints on his behaviour. But as long as men live a collective existence, their social lives are governed by a moral consensus, however relative and less than complete consensus may be. All social behaviour is normatively oriented, that is, given direction and definition by norms, rules of conduct that specify the "should" and "ought" of behaviour in social situations. Such norms are significant elements of culture.

Norms can obviously vary in their importance to the group in which they are held, and in the intensity by which they are believed in. Group life is built around conceptions of rights and privileges, obligations, and duties, all of which are morally significant to the group members. No sociological or psychological analysis of group life can, therefore, ignore the normative element in human behaviour. Norms are regulative and controlling standards that exist as shared moral expectations of behaviour; social order is necessarily moral order. When the moral standards are put into a written code, with specified punishment for violation, and social agencies are created to enforce them, these written rules constitute law. Law, in effect, is a body of institutionalised norms.

Social norms emerge out of the social interaction that creates a social order and are an integral part of that order. Like the very behaviour they serve to regulate, they are subject to change as new situations and problems develop for the group. Thus, however, sacred and reversed some norms may be for a social group, they are not immutable and internal, they change as does all life.

Culture

Taylor (1871) defined culture as "that complex whole which includes knowledge, belief, art, morals, law, customs, and any other capabilities and habits acquired by man as a member of society." But social scientists say that "everything is culture", for it has been defined to include all that man receives from previous generations as his social heritage. But as a definition, it does not suggest why man needs culture ? Perhaps to answer this Summer and Keller (1927) said that "culture is the means by which man adjusts to his environment." Social scientists have always defined, "Culture" as shared and as common to some group of people, and never a personal phenomenon. To Kluckhohn and Kelly (1945) "A culture is a historically created system of explicit and implicit designs for living, which tends to be shared by all or specially designated members of a group at a specified point in time."

The concept of culture is not remained static. It is to be expected in any scientific field that basic concepts are refined and redefined as changing usage and scientific developments alter their meaning and significance. But for the sociologist certain basic ideas about culture have persisted amid a matter of changing definitions. Parsons (1951) has noted three such ideas: "First, that culture is transmitted, it constitutes a heritage or a social tradition, secondly, that it is learned, it is not a manifestation, in particular content, of man's genetic constitution; and third, that it is shared." So culture is generated by men out of their interaction with one another; men create culture. Each generation takes its social heritage, uses it, and recreates it by adding new cultural elements before transmitting it to the next generation. In this way, culture changes as do human experiences. Talcott, Parsons and Kroeber (1958) include the above ideas and define culture as, "transmitted and created content and patterns of values, ideas, and other symbolic meaningful systems as factors in the shaping of human behaviour and the artifacts produced through behaviour." A definition similar in intent is somewhat differently worded is the one by Selznick and Selznick (1964) "Culture consists of everything that is produced by, and is capable of sustaining, shared symbolic experience."

All of the above definitions emphasize the symbol as basic to a conception of culture. Culture, then, has two divergent though related meanings. A still useful conception conceives of culture as encompassing the vast range of non-biological phenomenon that men themselves create and then transmit from one generation to another. It constitutes a social heritage, albeit an ever changing one. Another conception of culture places emphasis upon the fact that man organises his life and gives meaning and significance to it by means of symbols. It clearly implies that human beings desire to do more than organically survive. Through symbols people confer meaning upon their lives and construct a style of life. The values that they create are then used to interpret and organize their lives within the limits of objective contingencies and human power. Human beings, in essence, do not exist only biologically, they live by values and meanings expressed in symbols.

Social Values

Social values are a fundamental part of the cultural heritage of every society. They determine what the society considers important and what its members will defer. They define behaviour and determine whether or not a particular situation can be regarded as a social problem. Social problems exist in those areas of human relationship in which there is an awareness that individual and collective behaviour deviates from what is considered socially desirable and that calls for some sort of collective action.

Feeble-mindedness constitutes a social problem to that society which believes that inbreeding with the feeble-minded deteriorates the stock, physically, mentally or morally, and then permits them to die in consequence of an unmitigated struggle for existence contrary to humanitarian ideals. Pre-marital sexual behaviour is a social problem because it endangers the traditional value of chastity. Crime jeopardises the value attached to property and it threatens the collective security of the society from within. The care of the aged is, accordingly, a social problem if there are some who are in danger of dying from exposure and starvation in a society which looks upon death from these causes as undesirable. Divorce is a social problem in that society in which the ideal of marriage until terminated by death is considered basic to social welfare. Unemployment is a social problem because it threatens to make the unemployed depends upon others for support or die of starvation. Modern recreation is a social problem because it has become so commercialised that the primary motive of satisfying the genuine needs of man is felt to be sacrificed in the interest of commercial gain and exploitations. In these and many other respects, social values constitute the core of social organization; when these values change, social disorganization comes into existence. According to Thomas and Zmaniecki (1970), "Social disorganization becomes a social problem when changes arising from the conflict go on too rapidly so that the existing social structure is impaired in advance of the development of new elements to take the place of the old."

If society could be viewed for purposes of analysis as an organism, then it would follow logically that it could, like an organism, have a natural state of health and have a 'normal' condition. Any deviation from this is pathological, an abnormal state of the organism. Thus, social pathology signified an unhealthy state of the social organism, a sickness of society by virtue of some departure from what was normal and natural to society.

As evidence of social pathology, sociologists examined the lives of the immigrant poor in rapidly growing cities, the manner in which urbanisation, immigration and social mobility detached people from traditional social groups such as family and village. They looked at slums and poverty, crime and delinquency, desertion, divorce and the broken family, and ethnic conflict and these are labelled "social pathology". The concept of social pathology gave way in time to a concept of social disorganization. Thus, divorce and desertion served as indexes of the disorganization of the family. By implication, then, a presumed older stable pattern of family life was taken as the organization of the family, departure from which meant a disorganising process in the normal pattern of family life. In other problems the same assumption held: what had prevailed before but was undergoing change was labelled organization, and the departure from it was disorganization.

There were other difficulties with the concept of social disorganization. For one thing, the assumption of a previous state of organization much like the pathologist's assumption about a normal state of the social organism—then implied that the indexes of disorganization had only been observable in society when social disorganization occurred. And this process, it must be remembered, was linked to the rapid industrialization and urbanization of America; thus it was a historically recent event. But prostitution and crime, for example, were hardly a new phenomenon; rather there was good historical evidence of their having existed for as long as we have any adequate records. No sociologist was so simple to argue that recent social disorganization had created such social phenomena as crime, prostitution and divorce but he was prone to argue that it had produced a sharp increase. What before had been perceived as an occasional and individual problem now was perceived as frequent and common and thus a concern of the community.

So the society has its norms, values, culture, system etc. and the person who deviates from these is called deviant and becomes a social problem. Individuals as a rule are conformists, they like to think and act in such a way as to win the approval of the community to which they belong. They like to follow the existing customs, conventions and norms of their group. But occasionally we come across non-conformity. Rebels appear who delight in defying public opinion; such defiance is not necessarily wrong or anti-social. The preaching of the prophet, though in one sense rebellious, had a cathartic effect on his community. His rebellious message is really a clarion call to self-examination. Moderate drinking is neither atypical nor anti-social, but one who escapes from reality to a dream world created by drugs or drinks is certainly robbing society of his services. An able-bodied men who begs, is depriving the community of the benefits of eight manhours of work a day. Crime is obviously antisocial as it is the defiance of laws made for the protection of society. A man who steals acts contrary to the basic economic law that you must earn the bread you eat. He helps himself to it free of cost while the beggar cadges it on compassionate grounds. A class of people may behave in an atypical way, e.g. prostitutes. All these forms of anti-social behaviour collectively came under the heading of social pathology—personality disorganization.

Sociopathic behaviour was long considered only from the

moral point of view. No doubt this point of view is important and the psychologist does not want to underrate its significance. But there are other points of view also which need careful consideration. The social psychologist is more interested in knowing why such behaviour takes place, than in sitting in judgement over it. Generally speaking the late nineteenth and the early twentieth century sociologists grouped together under the heading of "social pathology" those human actions which run contrary to ideas of residential statility, property ownership, sobriety, thrift, habituation to work, small business enterprises, sexual discretion, family solidarity, neighbourliness and discipline of the will. In effect social problems were considered to be any form of behaviour violating the morals from which these ideals were projected.

Type of Disorganization

Social disorganization arises out of a breakdown in the functioning of parts of the cultural organization with reference to one another. Social disorganization is a situation in which attitudes and values are not in accord and the vital relationships of the social groups are thereby interrupted or dissolved. Without social values, neither social organization nor social disorganization would exist. Attitudes and values co-exist in a reciprocal fashion and one is dependent upon the other. Both reflect the changes in society and the disparities in social opinion. They reflect, in short, the degree of social disorganization.

The dynamic forces that bring about social disorganization also produce disorganization not only of the individual but also of the community. Crime, unemployment, venereal disease, divorce, illiteracy, sickness, insanity, drunkenness and suicide are all indices of different aspects of a disorganized society. Some of these relate primarily to the disorganization of the individual, others to that of the family, and still others to that of the local community.

In India, the transition from the rural to urban economy, from handicraft production to the machine industry has been too disintegrative and the growth of railways, cities and towns too rapid to permit a slow and gradual adaptation of the habits and attitudes of the people. Such changes have accompanied a severe economic pressure, the disruption of the joint family and caste control and the unsettlement of status and custom so that the individual has been thrown out of doors to the fury of economic forces. It is the failure of the mental and social adaptation that accounts for the prevalence and increase among the urban middle classes in India of such diseases as dyspepsia, diabetes, tuberculosis, hysteria and insanity and also of suicide, the continuous city-ward drift due to unremunerative agriculture, indebtedness and multiplication of agricultural labourers, and the overcrowding in our industrial cities and towns, have introduced new problems of moral and social deterioration unknown before. Intemperance and prostitution in all our industrial towns and cities are alike the results of a striking excess of males over females, overcrowding in slums, casual unemployment, uncertainty and mental depression.

Under personal disorganization are included crime in all its manifestations, drunkenness, beggars, criminals and prostitutions etc., which are briefly discussed below.

Alcoholism

The use of alcohol as a beverage is widespread in western civilization and, by the majority of the population at least, its use in moderation is generally approved. Where alcohol is consumed mainly for purposes of conviviality or ceremony it is termed social or controlled drinking; the social drinker is able to control his drinking and rarely becomes intoxicated. Drinkers who deviate from the norms of the drinking patterns of a culture and from such legal norms as those prohibiting drunkenness and driving while intoxicated, are referred to as excessive drinkers.

Excessive drinkers use alcohol for purposes of intoxication and some may even become completely dependent upon its effects. The heavy drinker uses alcohol more frequently than does the social drinker. He has occasional spress of drunkness, but in general his drinking does not seriously deviate from drinking norms. Alcoholics are those excessive drinkers who deviate markedly from drinking norms by the frequency and quantity of their consumption of alcohol and by the unconventional times and places selected for the drinking. Such excessive consumption of alcohol tends to disturb their interpersonal relationships in their family, occupational, and social groups. The alcoholic is unable to control consistently, or stop at will, either the start of drinking or its termination once started. Most deviant of all are those whose alcoholism has become chronic. Chronic alcoholic almost completely lose control over their drinking and become "compulsive" drinkers. They become so dependent upon alcohol that they live to drink and drink to live. Some of their characteristics are solitary drinking, morning drinking, and general physical deterioration.

Thus, alcoholism and drug addiction refer to the maladaptive consequences of the intake of alcohol and drugs motivated by compulsive drives and manifested through psychosocial disfunctioning. According to WHO Expert Committee (1958): drug-addiction is a state of periodic or chronic intoxication, detrimental to the individual and to society, produced by repeated consumption of a drink, either natural or synthetic. From the medical view-point addiction is a condition resulting from repeated use of any drug to the extent that continued use of it becomes essential in order to retain normal physiological functions and discontinuance of the drug causes definite physical and mental symptoms. It has three characteristics (a) overpowering desire or need to continue taking the drug and to obtain it by any means, (b) a tendency to increase the dose, and (c) a psychic, sometimes physical, dependence on the effects of the drug.

According to Keller (1972) "Alcoholism is a chronic behavioural disorder manifested by repeated drinking of alcoholic beverages in excess of the dietary and social uses of the community and to an extent that interferes with the drinker's health and of his social and economic functioning." There are people who consider alcoholism as vice. There are others who regard it as an illness. The latter position should be acceptable to us. The personality of an alcoholic often reveals unhappy childhood, personal frustrations, anxieties, and other factors of psysiological and sociological importance. Drinking may be occasional or regular. Owing to cultural pattern it may not be possible—not even desirable—to impose total prohibition on all drinks. Those who have become or are likely to get personally disorganized on account of drinking, constitute the main plank of our problem. Fanatic-obsscssive opposition to normal drinks seems more pathological than drinking itself. Today the use of alcohol represents a conflict of values, while excessive drinking and alcoholism may be considered as deviant behaviour. The value conflicts over the use of alcohol actually represents a struggle between a Calvinistic tradition that it is the community's responsibility to supervise the individual's drinking and an individualistic tradition that regards drinking as a matter of free choice. There is no question that the excessive use of alcoholic beverages is costing industry huge sums of money in the form of absenteeism, in efficiency on the job, and accidents. It is of course impossible to estimate the indirect social cost.

Physiological Effects of Alcohol

Alcohol is a chemical substance which is derived through a process of fermentation or by distillation. Although the process of distillation of alcoholic beverages from barley, corn, wheat, and other grains is fairly recent in human history, nearly all societies have made fermented beverages, such as wine, beer, end similar products, for thousands of years (Patrick, 1952). Following the intake of alcoholic beverages, a certain amount of alcohol is absorbed into the blood stream from the stomach, but most of it is absorbed in the small intestine. It is carried in the blood to the liver and then disseminated in diluted form to every part of the body. Because there can never be more than 1 per cent of alcohol in the blood stream, it cannot directly cause organic brain damage, neither "corroding", "dissolving" nor in any way directly harming the brain cells (McCarthy and Douglass, 1959). "Infact, all substances classed as volatile anesthetics, such as other, can produce precisely the same reactions upon the brain" (Haggard, 1945). Alcohol is not physiologically habit forming in the sense that certain narcotics are: one does not become a chronic drinker as the result of the first, twentinth, or even one hundredth drink. Moreover, it has never been demonstrated that the craving for alcohol is inherited (Roe, 1945).

Actually, the effect of alcohol is determined by the rate at which it is absorbed into the body, which depends upon the kind of alcoholic beverage consumed, the proportion of alcohol it contains, the speed with which it is drunk, and the amount and type of food in the stomach, as well as on certain minor physiological differences among individuals (McCarthy and Douglass, 1959). In moderate quantities, alcohol has relatively little effect on a person, but large quantities disturb the activity in the organs controlled by the brain and cause the phenomenon known as "drunkeness". If taken in moderate amounts, alcohol can lessen tensions and worry, and in general it may ease the fatigue associated with anxiety (Haggard, 1945). It presents an illusion of being a stimulant because it reduces or alters the cortical control and not from stimulation. Drinking plays a significant role in everyday interpersonal affairs. Alcohol is used by many people to celebrate national holidays, such as Christmas and New Year, and to rejoice in victories, whether those of war, the football field, or the ballot box.

There are several types of drinkers: the social or controlled drinkers, the heavy drinkers, the alcoholics, and the chronic alcoholics. A social or controlled drinker drinks for reasons of sociability, conviviality, and conventionality. He may or may not like the taste and effects produced by alcohol. Above all, else, he is able to desist from the use of intoxicating beverages when he chooses to do so. He drinks in a take-it-or-leave-it manner. There are two types of social drinkers, the occasional and the regular drinker. The former drinks sporadically and may have only a few drinks a year, where as the regular social drinker may drink three or more times a week.

Not only does the heavy drinker make more frequent use of alcohol than the regular social drinker, in addition and occasionally. He may consume such quantities that intoxication results. Some studies have defined a heavy drinker as one who takes three or more drinks of liquor at a "Sitting" more than once a week. He is sometimes, but not always, given to week-end-binges or at a party, may be drinking too heavily or just having a few more than anyone else in the place. Whatever else may be said about the excessive drinker, this type, in common with social drinkers, but with greater difficulty, may be able to curtail or completely cease drinking on his own volition. Depending upon circumstances, he may continue drinking in this manner for the rest of his life; he may later reduce the frequency and quantity of his alcohol consumption, or he may become an alcoholic.

Alcoholics are those whose frequent and repeated drinking of alcoholic beverages is in excess of the dietary and social usages of the community and is to such an extent that it interferes with health or social or economic functioning. The alcoholic is unable to control consistently, or to stop at will, either the start of drinking or its termination once started (Keller, 1958: 1960). Some of the elements in this definition are: (1) reliance on alcoholic beverages, (2) repetitiveness or chronicity of the drinking in the sense that the drinking does not take place on rare occasions, (3) ill effects which derive from the drinking and not from other causes. Drinking also affects the drinker's life and not just society. These ill effects may be either definite ill health, social or interpersonal ill effects, such as disruption of the family or ostracism which would not occur if the drinking were stopped, or economic effects, such as inability to keep a job, work efficiently, or take care of one's property as well as one could without the drinking.

Chronic alcoholics characteristically have a "Compulsion" to drink continually. Of particular importance are such other characteristics as solitary drinking, morning drinking, and general physical deterioration.

Personality Traits and Excessive Drinking

Why some social drinkers become excessive drinkers and some excessive drinkers develop into alcoholics is not entirely clear at the present time. Most psychiatrists believe that alcoholism is a consequence of personality maladjustment. According to this view, certain childhood experiences produce feelings of insecurity which, together with difficulties in interpersonal relationships of adult life, produce tensions and anxieties. Because the use of alcohol reduces anxiety, some persons may come to depend upon it. Over a period of years this dependence on alcohol as a way of escaping hidden or obvious difficulties with which the individual cannot deal increases.

The psychiatric explanation, although widely held, has several limitations. In the first place, such a theory is largely dependent for evidence on the personality traits of alcoholics and the differences between them and non-alcoholics. The personality traits of an alcoholic are measured after some ten to fifteen years of drinking in which the individual has usually had many problems due to his drinking, problems not only with his family but with his employer and others, and experiences which the non-alcoholic has probably not had.

Although efforts have been made to sketch an "alcoholic personality" presumably applicable to all alcoholics; more recent surveys have concluded that scientific reports to-date do not permit us to define such an alcoholic personality, or even to come to any substantial agreement as to what it might be like. In this connection Sutherland *et al.* (1950) found that the two groups (alcoholic and non-alcoholic) do not differ on personality traits. Moreover, it cannot be assumed that the personality traits displayed by the alcoholic were there before excessive drinking began. It is possible that a number of types, such as the person who takes pride in his ability to consume large quantities of alcohol without becoming drunk, have a susceptibility for alcoholism.

Group associations and cultural factors play an important part in determining who becomes an excessive drinker and who does not. There are differences not only in the drinking customs of societies but in those of subgroups within a modern society. Subgroups differ in the way in which alcohol is used, the extent of drinking, and altitudes towards drunkeness. The correlation of diverse drinking patterns with alcoholism can help us to test a number of hypothesis. Some believe that frequent drinking will lead to alcoholism. Yet those groups with relatively high frequency of drinking, such as the American jews, particularly the orthodox, and the Italian-American, have low rates of alcoholism (Synder, 1958). Drinking generally takes place in small groups, and within these groups drinking norms tend to develop; more than two-third of the drinking occasions among men, for example, in rural Finland involve groups of two to four persons (Kumari, 1957). Moreover, while conformity between drinking habits and drinking norms is the rule in small groups identification with a group is a variable on the basis of which it is possible to explain an individual's norms and his behaviour (Allardt, 1957). Drug takers were found to be passive and withdrawn while controls were more aggressive (Phillips, Phillips & Devidson, 1975).

Peneston (1978) worked out that Ss with low scores on the ego-strength scale had been drinking alcohol when they attempted suicide. Lindquist, Lindsay & White (1979) in a study of drug users and a college student group (N = 114), found that the drug users were less assertive, less socially assertive, and more socially anxious than non-addict populations. Fowler, Liskow and Tanna (1980) studied alcoholics with and without secondary depression and compared the two groups on a wide variety of clinical variables. Results indicate that the 20 Ss with secondary depression reported more fights, arrest, neurotic complains, suicidal behaviours and recent undesirable life events than Ss with alcoholism alone. Data indicate a close relationship between negative events and secondary depression of alcoholism. The finding suggest the subjects with secondary depression are at greater risk for suicidal the subjects without a depressive syndrome.

Class Differences in Excessive Drinking

Drinking customs and attitudes towards drinking vary in terms of the class structure. Dollard (1937) has shown, for example that in the upper classes both sexes drink a good deal, and their drinking generally does not involve a moral issue, provided it is done "properly". One is condemned in the upper classes, not for drinking, nor for drunkeness, but for anti-social acts while drunk. Fighting is taboo; aggressive behaviour is heavily penalized even when expressed only in verbal assaults. The lower-upper class is said to be distinguished from the other members of the upper class by the "Cocktail Set". In this particular group there is more alcoholic drinking in general and some excessive drinking which may result from the fact that the persons in the lower-upper class, in striving to reach the top of the social ladder feel more insecure. The role of the host varies with the structure of the cocktail party, the composition of the guests, and the objectives of the party (Riesman, 1960). Cocktail parties vary in the degree to which persons "responsible" for them can influence course. At the large urban cocktail party, for example, the host tends to be relatively powerless, for such parties most often lack formal structure. The array of guests is heterogeneous, consisting of a wide cross-section of persons of varying social statuses. Lack of space force persons into little clusters where they may offer bits of polite small talk. Other persons, whose isolation is concealed by the unstructured nature of the group, may find solace in the food and drink. Such parties as these cannot be described as purely "sociable" occasions; rather, they are often "coming out" parties for men, products, or ideas. Thus, the socially mobile couple who would not ordinarily give such a party, because of their lack of money and experience, may find themselves in a position which demands that they preside over such an affair.

On the upper-middle rungs of the success ladder, men drink at social, gatherings and for business reasons. Women generally refrain from much drinking, however, and on the whole there seems to be neutral attitude towards the consumption of liquor. Drinking parties seem to be increasing among middle-class groups who find escape, relaxation, and release through alcohol. A study (Clinard, 1963) of drinking parties, as compared with non-drinking parties, revealed that they were attended by white-collar groups who, among the men, found increasing tensions in the insecurity of their status in an era of high-speed industrial and commercial activity and high pressure salesmanship (Robinson, 1942). Members of the lower-middle class striving desperately for recognition and status, and, in fact, for anything which would widen the gap between them and those whom they consider lower than themselves, have strong taboos against drinking, particularly among the women, because excessive drinking is associated in their minds with the behaviour of the lower classes.

According to Dollard (1937), the lower classes, in contrast to the lower-middle class, often do not exert restraints on drinking where both men and women may consume alcoholic beverage.

Occupation and Excessive Drinking

Social patterns call for more immoderate drinking in certain occupational categories than in others. This view has been supported by the finding that a heavy disproportion of alcoholic psychoses are found in jobs with relatively low income and prestige, a result of the acceptance of heavy drinking as a norm in certain lower-class occupational groups (Robert, 1949). On the other hand, McCord and McCord (1964) after studying a group of 254 persons, found that middle-class Americans were significantly more prone to alcoholism than were members of the lower class.

The Army, the Navy, the salesmen and seamen away from home, all are rich in drinking culture. In these groups the harsh, the monotonous and the protective but controlled routines are broken by the nights, weekends and lay-offs which offer opportunities to drink. Fantasy around future drinking episodes serves the function of reducing the impact of heavy jobs in heat and cold, and of alleviating dull routines, sexual deprivation, and the loneliness of the all-male groups. Drinking becomes a symbol of manliness and gioups integration (Pittman & Gordon, 1964).

Beggars

Of all social evils today begging is perhaps the most demoralising. It constitutes a very complex socio-economic problem. In fact all socio-economic changes are accompanied with begging. Today the problem of begging is very acute. Probably India is the only country in the world where about five million beggars wander about the streets with perfect freedom, living on the spontaneous, unorganized charity of the individual citizen. Half of them are able-bodied making on an average more income than the wages of millions of poor peasants and workers. That is because a large section of the population considers giving money to the beggars as absolution of their sins.

Firstly, we have to know who is a beggar ? and what is begging? The beggar in England is described as consisting of "every person wandering abroad or placing himself or herself in any public place, street, highway, court or passage, to beg or gather alms, or causing or procuring any child or children (under 16) to do so (Memoria, 1970). It also comprises every person wandering abroad and endeavouring, by exposure of wounds or deformities, to obtain or gather alms or endeavouring to procure charitable contributions of any nature or kind, under false or fraudulent pretence. In India "a person who has no ostensible means of subsistence or who cannot give a satisfactory account of himself is regarded as a destitute, vagrant or a beggar" (Criminal Procedure Code, Section 55(1). Different Indian states have enacted laws to define vagrancy or beggary and take steps to prevent this social evil. According to the Bengal Vagrancy Act (VII of 1943) "vagrant means a person asking for alms in any public place or remaining in any public place or wandering about in such a condition or manner as makes it likely that he exists by asking for alms". Similarly, the Bombay Beggars Act (XXIII of 1945) stipulates that "a person without means of subsistence and wandering about or found in public places or allowing himself to be used as an exhibit for the purpose of begging is covered by the definition. The Bihar Prevention of Beggary Act (I of 1952) provides that "soliciting alms in a public place including a place of worship whether or not under any pretence, entering any private premises for such purpose, exposing or exhibiting any sore, wound, injury, deformity or disease whether of human being or animal for such purpose or for extorting alms, having no visible means of subsistence, wandering about making it likely that the person exists by soliciting alms, allowing himself to be used for such purpose."

The Children Act, 1960, passed by the Indian Parliament, defines beggary as "soliciting or receiving alms in a public place or entering on any private premises for the purposes of soliciting or receiving alms, whether under the pretence of singing, dancing, fortune-telling performing tricks or selling articles or otherwise exposing or exhibiting with the object of obtaining or extorting alms, any sore, wound, injury, deformity or disease, whether of himself or of any other person or of an animal, allowing oneself to be used as an exhibit for the purpose of soliciting or receiving alms (Chandra, 1967). Begging can also be understood as a deviation from the norm that one should work for one's livelihood. But when one deviates from this norm and lives on alms he is known as a beggar. A large number of beggars is a threat to this norm. It means non-utilization of available human energy and also a drag upon the existing resources of our society.

Begging is a pattern of human behaviour which can be understood in terms of a combination of circumstances peculiar to the life of a particular individual. The existence of begging depends in part upon the factors which stimulate individuals to commit offences and in part upon the opportunities that society presents for begging as well as the social tolerance. An act of begging can be analysed into two component parts—asking and giving. Both of them are closely interrelated yet the attitude of the society to each of them varies greatly. "Giving" is encouraged, but "asking" is discouraged and as to ask for one's livelihood has been considered worst among all the professions. Thus, society has an ambivalent attitude towards begging. Since "asking" requires that a beggar should be in need, he devises certain methods that create maximum sympathy. His motive is to get the maximum he can from a giver. "Giving" is a complex phenomena; one may give out of sympathy or as a duty feeling.

In Western countries begging is not as acute a problem as it is in India. Begging is a symptom of social disorganization and the widespread custom of alms-giving by individuals and institutions is the method by which the disability, helplessness or social inadequacy of the beggars has been sought to be mitigated in India.

Many types of beggars exist in India. The layman usually associates the idea of begging with the unutterably poor, the disabled, the blind, the crippled and the diseased who seek assistance or charitable contributions. Tucker (1970) divided beggars into three groups, hobes, tramps and bums. He explained that a hobo is a migratory worker. A tramp is a migratory non-worker. And a bum is a stationary non-worker. Kumarappa (1945) classified beggars as follows:

(a) The child beggar, who may be paid or unpaid assistant of the adult beggar.
(b) The physically defectives, including the blind, the deaf mute, the crippled, the maimed and deformed.
(c) The mentally defectives, including a large proportion of the destitutes, immoral, delinquent and criminal population.
(d) The diseased persons, suffering from infectious diseases such as leprosy, epilepsy, T.B. and skin diseases, with sores and ulcers, covered with plasters on which myriads of flies settle and feed.
(e) The able-bodied, who consider begging their birth-right and bully, harass and trouble the public into giving them alms, and who are lazy and roam about in the cities. They beg by day and turn into thieves and robbers by night.
(f) The religious mendicants, so familiar in the figure of the *Sanyasi*, the *Yogi*, the *Sadhu*, the *Vairagi*, the *Fakir* etc.
(g) The bogus mendicants, who are able-bodied laymen and who have no affiliation with any religious order whatever but like to get on without work, and profit by the generosity of the unsuspecting and religiously minded orthodox people.

(h) The tribal beggars, who move about from place to place singing and reciting local songs and begging.
(i) The employed beggars are the persons who work in night shifts in mills and factories and go out begging during the day.

The beggar nuisance is more localised in big cities, in railway stations, in pilgrim centres, at fairs and festivals, where large congregations of people occur, and even in some villages. A committee in Mysore which examined the beggar problem in 1943 reported that:

(a) There were more beggars in cities than in villages.
(b) Their numbers had abnormally increased between the year 1935 to 1941.
(c) Some were diseased and physically disabled.
(d) A good number of them were able-bodied.
(e) A decent number of beggars were below 19 years of age.
(f) To a majority of them, this was the sole means of living while to a few it was a supplement to income from other sources.
(g) Many of the beggars were literate, had passed examinations, were artisans and workers and yet had taken to begging.
(h) They married and multiplied, thus creating hereditary beggars.

According to the Census Report for 1951, the total number of beggars and vagrants was 4,87,907 of which there were 3,44,216 males and 1,43,641 females. The Planning Commission in 1963 estimated it to be 20 lakh. But recent estimates put the figure at 50 lakh for India but the figure may well be above 60 lakh (Jha, 1987).

The Madras School of Social Work made a survey of the beggar problem in November 1953 and enumerated 7,443 beggars. The survey disclosed an alarming number of able-bodied beggars (4,396), and even more significant was the fact that 1888 children were under the age of 12 years. Diseased numbered 1154; disabled 1435 and insane 459; leprosy patients 211; blind 179; crippled 134 and afflicted with elephantiasis 110.

The methods of begging were also listed as: ordinary 4663, exhibiting wounds 765, exhibiting new-born babies 669, singing 658, religious 509, exhibiting pregnancy 131 and exhibiting dead bodies.

Favourite places of begging were listed as: pavements 3066, temples 985, bus stops 851, hotels 686, markets 546, railway stations 375 and parks 221.

A survey of beggars (Ratan, 1961) was conducted in Kanpur. He reports that out of a total population of about 28,000 beggars in the urban areas of U.P., there were 3,217 beggars in Kanpur. The number of beggars in the city was as high as 12 per cent of the total number of beggars in urban areas. About 48 per cent were concentrated on various Ghats of the Ganga. It was estimated sometime back that Bombay alone has more than 60,000 beggars, Calcutta 35,000 and Delhi 12,000. According to a senior officer of the Welfare Department, this figure is 5,000 for Patna (Jha, 1987). Of the total number of beggars, 911 were below 20 years of age, 1,540 between 20 and 50 years, 592 between 51 and 70 years, while 162 beggars were between 71 and 100 years of age.

According to a recent survey (Jha, 1987) conducted in Kanpur, the average monthly income of the beggar ranged from Rs. 30 to Rs. 15) per month, in cash including what they procured in cereals, sweets and fruits. The bulk of them earned in the range of Rs. 75 to Rs. 90 per month. Many female beggars did not depend only on alms, but also made money through immoral means. Several young female beggars had one to three children, whose percentage remained shrouded in mystery. Amarchand Bhatia (Kimarappa, 1945) has drawn our attention to one special feature of the life of beggars in India-organization. Beggar organizations "aim at joint begging, pooling of all resources accumulated through individual or group begging, joint cooperative household and joint worship of a 'Guru'. They maintain fraternal relationship among beggars coming from a particular part of the country for the purpose of joint defence against lawful forces of the Government and seek not only to minimize the toe-trouble engendered by individual endeavours but also to eliminate inimical individuals from within its rank and tile. Some of these organizations are loose and casual which scatter easily and willingly and break many a time within a year but again come into formation according to the exigencies of time. Others are very strong, powerful, self-supporting, self-determining, authoritarian, regional, and communal. Only very hard knock can mash and disintegrate them.

Beggary is a joint product of both the social situation and the economic condition of the country. Moorthy (Jha, 1987) in a survey of beggars in Bombay found that the reason behind beggary may be many. But morons, sexual perverts and emotionally unstable persons from a high proportion of the beggar population in every city in India. There are also the borderline cases of half normal and half abnormal or subnormal individuals who fail to obtain a satisfactory social adjustment. Some are ugly-looking or have suffered from hideous sores that have subjected them to public jesting and bullying from childhood. Rebuffs have driven such frustrated individuals to the underworld where they obtain status. All such individuals show major emotional disturbances that have made them misfits in their families and social situations and driven them to the life of begging. Unremunerative agriculture, famine, flood, epidemics, poverty, unguided childhood, unemployment and disruption of joint family and of caste control are the major causes of increasing the rate of beggary in India. There is a prevailing belief among us that the beggars are the outcome of our poverty, until it is cured, beggary will prevail. But a prominent social scientist, Gokhale (Jha, 1987) rejects this notion. "All beggars are not poor and all the poor are not beggars, he says. Begging may be misfortune but it is an offence if misfortune is exploited."

Criminal

Crime is a form of behaviour that society refuses to tolerate. The tolerance level differs from one society to another to such an extent that crime itself becomes a relative term. Although it affects everyone, few people are fully aware of its implications. Its far-reaching consequences may be viewed from two aspects, the criminal and his victim, i.e. the problem of crime can be regarded both from the standpoint of the individual and that of the society. Crime as a social act is nothing more than a "failure or refusal to live up to the standard of conduct deemed binding by the rest of the community" or "some act or omission in respect of which legal punishment may be inflicted on the person who is in default whether by acting or omitting to act." The word 'Crime' is born of Latin "Crimen" which means 'charge' or 'offence'. The *Waverley Encyclopaedia* defines it as "An act forbidden by law, and for performing which the perpetrator is liable to punishment". Both the young and juvenile offenders who disturb the society by their unsocial acts fall within the category of disorganized group. Crime is committed by criminals and the criminals are human beings who, for whatever reasons, are motivated to act in the ways which the law condemns. It is endemic throughout the world. It not only costs millions of rupees every year but represents also an even greater loss in terms of human happiness and human welfare. So it is the problem of the whole society. Thus it is a socio-economic concept and linked with the social norms. Social customs and conventions vary from country to country and crime is to be always judged against this background. Another relevant factor is circumstance; what is criminal under certain circumstances becomes laudable under certain others. Telling lies normally considered to be highly reprehensible is tolerated and even praised during war times, if they are told out of patriotic motives and with the intention of misleading the enemy. Head-hunting is encouraged in certain tribes, though civilized society is horrified by murder. The *Concise Encyclopaedia of Crime and Criminals* (1961) has defined 'crime' thus: "A crime is an act or default which prejudices the interests of the community and is forbidden by law under pain of punishment."

Gillin (1946) has tried to define crime as "an act that has been shown to be actually harmful to society, or that is believed to be socially harmful by a group of people that has the power to enforce its beliefs and that places such an act under the ban of positive penalties." According to Tappan (1947) "crime is an intentional act in violence of the Criminal Law, committed without defuse or excuse, and penalised by the State as a felony or misdemeanour." For our purposes, a criminal is an anti-social parasite, one who behaves in ways which are so contrary to those morals of his society which have to do with rights of persons or of property, that he is a hazard to the welfare of the community whether or not his behaviour is known to the members of the community (Lapiere and Farnsworth, 1949). In terms of legal interpretation crime is defined by William Blackstone (1972) as "an act committed or omitted, in violation of a public law either forbidding or commanding it." Landis and Landis (1972) hold that "crime is an act which the State has declared harmful to group welfare and for which the State has power to punish." From the social point of view Sutherland (1974) opined that "criminal behaviour is that behaviour in violation of the criminal law." Elliot and Meirill (1972) explain that "a crime is an act prohibited by law which may be punished by death or by fine or by imprisonment in jail, work houses, reformatory or prison." Psychologically speaking, a criminal can even be looked upon as a sick person and the causes of his anti-social behaviour and tendencies may be found in his person. Though, he holds the strings of many lives in his hands, in the long run it is the criminal himself who suffers much more than the society. He is hated, persecuted, despised and is thrown out of the social arena, and finally put behind bars. When a criminal is sentenced to imprisonment, he is segregated not only from his family and friends, but also from the community, to which he essentially belongs. Horrocks (1964) said that "crime is a social cancer, and like its biological counterpart, it flourishes among and involves in one way or another all who comprise the society in which it occurs."

It is essential to understand the inner pressures operating on the criminal in various life situations which distort his responses. Under this inner pressure he perceives the environment, and as the researchers on the need and dynamic aspect of perception have amply demonstrated, the perceived world is altered to suit his needs (Bruner and Goodman, 1947; Lewiu, Chein and Murphy, 1942; McClleland and Liverman, 1949). If the way the individual perceived the situation is not taken into account his behaviour may appear meaningless and silly.

All the facts of modern psychology lead to the conclusion that behaviour at any moment is the product of a great number of contributing circumstances both within and without the individual and that in no sense is he entirely free to choose his actions. It is also true of the individual's desire which is a product of the interaction of internal and external forces. Criminal behaviour is then not to be looked upon as separate entity, or functionally autonomous. It is to be viewed as a mechanism of adjustment adopted by the individual style of life which he develops to meet the demands of his environments in terms of his perceptual and emotional reactions. "From the psychological point of view, criminal behaviour does not differ from normal behaviour and is, therefore, subject to the same laws of cause and effect" (Poffenberger, 1961). The resulting behaviour may be an approved one or a disapproved one, but it is natural for him at that time. From a psychological standpoint this behaviour is understandable. When one person kills another person, we generally do not approve of such behaviour. But in order to understand how it happened that the first person killed the second, we will have to fully comprehend the perceptions of the first man to understand his behaviour, i.e. to find out the purpose and meaning of criminal behaviour.

The growing complexities of life and living create an increasing number of problems, which demand the application of the highest capabilities and resources to solve them. In a society, as that of ours, marked with intense competition, conflicts, disappointment, frustrations and insecurity, crime is inevitable. Individuals are impelled to crime by feelings which have their origins in frustrations and disappointments. So long as people are frustrated, maladjustments are bound to occur and 'general criminal behaviour' is 'defective adjustment' (Hentic, 1947). Any force which obstructs adjustment is a force conducive to criminality. Whenever full expression of the motive is obstructed, adjustment is jeopardized. Inner strivings and motives that permit a person to live at peace with himself and his social group make for adjustment; those that create personal discord and social conflict favour maladjustment. Whether an individual is adjusted or maladjusted, besides other things, (extent of harmony among his manifold drives, motives and ideals, extent to which his wishes and aspirations are adequately attended), depends in a large measure on the extent to which his desires and actions are in conformity with the demands and standards of his social group. Criminals are basically non-conformists. They show utter disregard for socially approved ways in the attainment of their goals. Lack of respect for social and moral codes, is a symptom of maladjustment and indicative of conflict.

In recent years the increase in the extent of crime is appalling. Crimes has increased much faster than did the population. The alarming increase of crime is an indication of social maladjustment which is more prevalent in periods and regions of rapid change and many countries of the world are undergoing a rapid change. New heights of exploitations of the natural energies and resources are being touched. World-wide Industrialization and urbanization exhibit the same features of unwholesome congestion, loss of privacy, crime, delinquency, rising cost of living, population migrating to cities in search of jobs and better life, facility of communication, breaking of the joint family system and like everywhere including even the ecological patterns of distribution of criminals and delinquents and their anti-social behaviour. In short, our society is experiencing changes of indescribable nature. Social change and reconstruction have bright as well as dark spots. On the one hand they provide new heights of physical and material development, and on the other, their harmful consequences in the shape of crimes and criminals, unemployment, disabled and handicapped, rise sharply. In this sense crime may be regarded as an index of social progress and the price of social change.

Criminal Personality

There are delinquents and criminals and naturally each has a personality, normal or abnormal. But all the attempts to establish a distinct delinquent or criminal type have eventually come to naught. It is no longer correct to search for obvious physical defects that stigmatize the criminals. The majority of the criminals are not different physically from the normal individuals. Lambroso (1911) showed that the typical criminal possessed certain definite physical characteristics or anomalies such as slanting forehead, flattened nose, long ear lobes, a large jaw with no chin, heavy supraorbital ridges, either excessive hairiness or an abnormal absence of hair and an extreme sensitivity or non-sensitivity to pain. Kretschmer (1925) classified human beings into three rather different physical types and espoused body build as a correlative of behaviour. Since then Sheldon (1940) has elaborated the general thesis of Lombroso and Kretschmer. According to him the behaviour and personality are closely related to the structure of body. His three body types—endomorph, mesomorph, and ectomorph—are connected with the psychological temperamental type of viscerotonia, somatotonia and cerebrotonia successively. The somatotonia physical characteristic and the culture interact to produce deviant behaviour. The somatotonic is assertive and energetic, loves physical adventure, exercise, domination and power, likes to take risks and chances, is physically courageous, aggressive and psychologically callous. He is rather ruthless, unrestrained, indifferent to pain, generally noisy and also extroverted. Sheldon (1949) has found the delinquents and criminals to be heavy, insensitive, aggressive mesomorph. Sheldon and his co-workers have found support in the work of Gluecks (1956) who have concluded that body-build plays greater role in precipitating delinquent behaviour than has heretofore beer acknowledged. Argyle (1964) has reported that the delinquents differ physiologically. He reported that due to strong theta rhythm the individual becomes delinquents. Gluecks (1960) found that the delinquents as a group are distinguishable from the non-delinquents: (1) physically, in being essentially mesomorphic in constitution; (2) tempramentally, in being restlessly energetic, impulsive, extroverted, aggressive, destructive traits which may be related more or less to the erratic growth pattern and its physiologic correlates or consequences; (3) in attitude, being hostile, defiant, resentful, suspicious, stubborn, socially assertive, adventurous, unconventional non-submissive to authority; (4) psychologically, intending to be direct and concrete, rather than symbolic in intellectual expression, and in being less methodical in their approach to problem; (5) socio-culturally, in having been reared to a far greater extent than the control group in homes, of little understanding, affection, stability or moral fibre by parents usually unfit to be effective guides and protectors or, according to psychoanalytic theory desirable sources for emulation and the construction of a consistent, well-balanced, and socially normal super-ego during the early stages of character development. A study done by Laufer (1980) on a typological and demographic investigation. Characteristics of 201 criminals using, the Vocational Preference Inventory. The effectiveness of 3 criminal typologies and demographic information in differentiating and predicting levels of vocational interest was investigated. Results suggest that criminals express moderate interest in traditional occupations and have a differentiated set of vocational interests.

The vast majority of criminalities and delinquencies are impulsive acts or efforts to achieve financial gain, personal status, or some similar objective. Such people are conscious of their wrong doing, which ordinarily is accompanied by some degree of anxiety and feeling of guilt. There are several major difficulties in distinguishing between the personality traits of criminals and those of non-criminals. It may be that experiences, such as arrests, court appearances or imprisonment, may so affect the personality traits of criminals that it is impossible to determine what they were like prior to such experiences. Schuessler and Cressey (1950) reviewed a large number of studies of personality characteristics of delinquents and criminals. They made 113 comparisons, 42 per cent of the studies showed differences in favour of the non-delinquents and non-criminals, while the remainders were indeterminate. The doubtful validity of many of the obtained differences as well as the lack of consistency in the combined results makes it impossible to conclude from these data that criminality and personality elements are associated. Miksik (1978) found that persons who are anxious and depressive in nature are hypersensitive, lowered self-confidence, pessimism, depressive behaviour patterns and a more feminine attitude towards stressful situation.

One theory of the relation of personality traits and certain criminal behaviour needs more detailed analysis. The literature of many phases of deviant behaviour has had reference to the existence of a deviant personality type termed as criminal psychopathy personality, a habitual anti-social deviant (Harrison Gough, 1948). It has been suggested that normally all sexual offenders are psychopaths, or that the prison population is composed partly of psychopaths. Gilpin (1980) suggested that children be differentiated from anti-social personalities on the basis of superego development.

Wittels (1948) found that most of the sex killers are psychopathic personalities. No one knows or can even closely estimate how many such creatures there are, but at least tens of thousands of them are loose in the country today. Cleckley (1948) said that psychopaths repeat apparently purposeless thefts, forgeries, bigamies, swindlings, distasteful or indecent acts in public scores of times.

People believe that the concept of a psychopaths is real and that such a personality type sufficiently explains numerous anti-social acts (Throne & Pishkin, 1975). Saklofake and Eysenck (1980) studied personality and anti-social behaviour in delinquent and non-delinquent boys, and found that there was a significant difference between delinquents and badly behaved subjects. Also well-behaved subjects differed from the other group in anti-social behaviour and, in addition, from the badly behaved Ss on extraversion and from the delinquents on tough-mindness (psychoticism). On a scale of criminal prospensity, well behaved Ss were again significantly differentiated from both of the other groups.

Now we turn to analyse very briefly the factors responsible for criminality. In general, a situational perspective assumes that the causal process operating in some instance of criminality grind out of events closely tied in location and time to the deviant act. According to Sutherland (1974) 'The objective situation is important to criminality largely to the extent that it provides an opportunity for a criminal act. In his view, different persons will define the same objective situation differently, for someone the situations are conducive to criminality, but for others they are not. Thus only individuals motivated to engage in criminality will do so when confronted by particular situations. Sutherland (1968) overstated the matter by assuming that the earlier life experiences of offenders, extending over a lengthy time period, are always implicated in criminality. Contrary to his assumption, a long-term genetic process may not always operate with situational elements to create current lawbreaking. In many cases, criminality may be a response to nothing more temporal than the provocations and aberrations bound up in the immediate circumstances out of which deviant acts arise. Supporting this view Rizfo (1982) said that criminals are not in normal positions they suffer from mental illness.

Clearly for some instances of criminality, historical or genetic facts are quite powerful and situational elements are of minor significance, such as certain types of deviant sexual conduct involving exhibitionism, voyeurism, or pronounced sexually aggressive acts. Aggressive law breaking often labelled "Psychopathic" appears to be another form of criminality arising out of genetic factors, in this case, severe and early parental rejection. Thus some forms of criminal behaviour involve a heavy component of genetic etiology, whereas situational elements loom large in others. However, in many instances genetic factors and situational contingencies are both significant.

The family is an important force in adult criminality, but for somewhat different reasons. Some forms of adult law-breaking may result from distortions and pathologies in the offender's childhood experiences in his family. But nearly all adult persons eventually leave the family of orientation or parental family situation and move into a marriage, where they become engaged in the creation and maintenance of a new family system. The

Glueck's study (1952) of 500 delinquents and 500 non-offenders represents a major source of data regarding home factors. From this research, they reported that 49.8 per cent of the delinquents but only 28.8 per cent of the non-offenders were from broken homes. Moreover, 60.4 per cent of the delinquents and 34.2 per cent of the non-delinquents had at some time prior to the study lived in a home broken by separation, divorce, death or prolonged absence of one parent. The offenders were more commonly from homes in which the parents had a history of serious physical ailments, mental retardation, emotional disturbance, drunkenness or criminality. According to Gluecks, the parents of the delinquents were not good managers of income, were relatively poor planners of home routine, and exhibited less self-respect than parents of the non-offenders. Some parents were less ambitious, had poorer conduct standards, and poorer conjugal relations. The mothers of the delinquents gave poor supervision to their children and the parents showed less cohesiveness than did those of non-delinquents. Thus the defective patterns represent the major causal dimension in delinquency. Shaw and McKay (1931) and Reiss (1951) also supported the Glueck's view. Singh (1981) hypothesized that criminals would show a lower home, health, occupational, social, and emotional adjustment level when compared to non-criminals, and his results confirm the hypothesis. Also Buikhuisen (1982) discusses three basic principles used in studying criminals' behaviour: (1) all behaviour is a function of individual characteristic and situational factors; (2) all behaviours should be from a developmental perspective; and (3) different categories of behaviour ask for different explanations. And found that many items that are supposed to be characteristic of persistent offenders and identifying this cognitive dysfunction at an early age is extremely important.

On the basis of the above analysis, we may conclude that the influence of family patterns on delinquent conduct cannot be denied. However, to argue that family variables always have primacy over other factors would be to draw a caricature of real life. Claims that some particular family pattern is found in all forms of criminality are equally erroneous. Parental influences may well vary in significance in different types of criminality, just as particular factors or marital relationships important in one type of divorce may not be significant in another.

Prostitution

With the growth of civilization, several sociological problems have arisen of which prostitution or sexual promiscuity is one. Its origin is shrouded in mystery yet it is believed to be an ancient evil. It has existed to ever since and everywhere the men have lived in a community. Prostitution has existed in India since long and is referred to in the Vedas. It seems to have become a legalised institution only in the post-Vedic period. During this period the Aryans spread over a vast stretch of land and established several kingdoms in Northern India. Well settled in prosperous kingdoms they took to easy and luxurious life. Consequently, several small kingdoms became seats of pomp and luxury and the princes and princelings extended their liberal patronage to courtesans. These women added splendour to their courts, and during festivals, they enhanced the mirth by musical and dancing performances.

Apart from kings, there were other rich and prosperous individuals also who engaged the services of professional women. To meet this demand, a constant supply of women was needed and a regular trade in women developed. All medieval travellers who visited Indian cities were struck by the number of courtesans in them. Thus the prostitution has been the bane of society for so long that it has naturally engendered speculations about its causes and consequences.

The question what is prostitution and who are prostitutes has remained unresolved. Since different people have defined them in various ways, and these definitions have differed from time to time and from culture to culture. According to the *International Encyclopaedia of Social Sciences*, "prostitution is the granting of sexual access on a relatively indiscriminate basis for payment either in money or in goods, depending on the complexity of the local economic system. Payment is acknowledged to be for a specific sexual performance" (Sills, 1968). Normally prostitution is an act of sexual intercourse characterised by barter, promiscuity and emotional indifference.

The Suppression of Immoral Traffic in Women and Girls Act, 1956, defines the prostitute as "a female who offers her body for promiscuous sexual intercourse for hire whether in money or in kind". According to Puneckar and Rao (1967), "a prostitute is a female who habitually offers her body to any person other than the man to whom she is legally married for sexual intercourse or other substitute gratification for a consideration in cash or in kind." Article 3 of the new Constitution of the International Abolitionist Federation defines prostitution as "a habitual activity which in the case of a person, whether man or woman, consists in offering himself or herself for sexual purposes, to any other person, who may be prepared to pay for this in some form or other" (Pignier, 1972). A proposed amendment to it reads: "a girl or woman who offers her body to indiscriminate sexual intercourse especially for hire (Lall, 1970). Elloit and Merrill (1950) define prostitution as "an illicit sex union on a promiscuous and mercenery basis with accompanying emotional indifference. Thus prostitution is generally characterised by three criteria: (1) promiscuity, baser and emotional indifference, (2) it is different from the broader concept of sexual immorality due to the commercial nature of the relationship, (3) it is distinguished from illegitimacy which inevitably involves on illicit sex relationship but refers particularly to the production of a child outside the socially approved reproduction.

This promiscuous sexual intercourse is a great social evil.

The woman not only sells her body as a piece of precious ware to the public, whosoever is able to pay for it, but also perpetuates her criminalities against society, by inducing, kidnapping or by various other subtle means of procuring young innocent children and girls to make her trade prosperous and profitable. The extramarital excursion facilitates the breakup of marriage and happy family life. It wrecks personality and communicates diseases. And as such it has always been looked down upon with stigma by the social workers and reformers. Yet the wonder is that the institution of prostitution and of sexual traffic, reproved by morality, has existed throughout the centuries and amongst all the people. It is as ancient as the world and is probably one of the oldest professions in the world.

It is not only an urban problem but is observable in rural areas also in almost all countries. The form taken by it in rural areas is the reception of man in her house by one woman or by a woman and her daughter. Another form is the exploitation of village girls by the middleman who lure them for purposes of prostitution. Soliciting is not usually possible in the countryside. Keeping of large brothels and clandestine prostitution is typical of large cities and industrial centres.

Forms and Types of Prostitution

Commercialized prostitution is practised, at present, in various ways, e.g.:

(1) **Common Prostitutes:** The brothels and dens are main trained either by old prostitutes or men procurers who engage young girls in the age group of 16 to 20, majority of them being girls between 14 and 16 for it is youth and virginity that is most in demand in prostitution.

(2) **Amateures or Hotel Prostitutes:** Hotel prostitution has now become much more common. Hotel keepers engage girls of easy virtue, who live in private houses,

are educated, pleasure seeking and luxury-loving girls, and a number of them belong to decent and respectable homes and generally gainfully employed. These include college girls, telephone girl operators, stenos, society girls, etc. They are also called "call girls". They take to this occupation as secondary job to supplement their earnings.

(3) **Decentralized Prostitutes:** After the passage of the Suppression of Immoral Traffic Act, a certain amount of decentralization of prostitutes is found in different parts of the cities. With the liquidation of brothels, prostitutes have filtered into different localities wherein they carry on their trade independently.

(4) **Hereditary Prostitutes:** Both among the Hindu and Muslim communities there is a class of hereditary prostitutes. They are a heritage from the Mughal period. In them prostitution is handed down from mother to daughter as a profession with no shame attaching to a life of immorality. They know the art of singing and dancing and also train their girls in these arts from their childhood.

(5) **Prostitutes Belonging to Backward and Criminal Tribes:** In this category many gipsy-like nomadik tribes prostitute their girls as a matter of custom, such as the Nutts, Berias, Dhairs, Kanjars, Sansis and several others in the North, and Basavis, Koyis, Bediyas, Kolhatis, Harmis, Berads, Mang Garuds, Dombars etc. in the South.

(6) **Religious Prostitutes:** The Devdasi system still prevails in the South. In Karwar, in Orissa and in Mysore the practice of dedicating girls to temples continues particularly among the Harijans. Their duties are to dance in the temple before the Idol on ceremonial occasions.

(7) **Traditional Prostitutes:** This type and group of prostitutes is found around the places of the former Rajas,

Jagirdars and the rich. They were known as Kalavanthis, Nityamanglis or Manglamukhis.

(8) **Victims of Social and Sociological Conditions:** Besides the above types of prostitutes, there are many prostitutes who are recruited from poor but respectable families. Among there are:
   (a) women who, due to unemployment and economic necessity, have been driven to prostitution.
   (b) young widows, who are made to feel that they are a burden on their families.
   (c) to some extent, old maidens and enforced widows; they provide a rich ground for recruitment to the field of prostitution.
   (d) ill-treated wives often compelled either to end their life or to leave the house in sheer desperation.
   (e) unprotected and destitute girls who perhaps had been taken advantage of by members of their own families or been seduced or abducted by outsiders or exposed to immoral influences.

(9) **Foreign Prostitutes:** In the port towns and large cities of the country are to be found a host of Chinese, Japanese, Jewish, Arab, Anglo-Indian, French and Persian prostitutes who cater to the needs of the high class gentry.

Factors Responsible for Prostitution

From the male point of view the causes of prostitution lie in unfulfilled sexual urges and the social barriers to their satisfaction. Broadly speaking, prostitution has its roots in "personal" and "impersonal" factors. The personal factors are those which grow out of man's biological nature and the expression of this urge takes in human relationships. The impersonal factors include those broad socio-economic relationships which initiate and virtually institutionalize prostitution in our social organization.

But girls may accept such a profession under so many circumstances such as:

(1) **Poverty and hunger:** According to the survey report of the Committee on Social and Moral Hygiene (1958), poverty and lack of employment opportunity are the biggest factor (55.4%) followed by domestic failure (22.7%). The percentage was 41 per cent in a sample survey undertaken by Shri Kanga (Mamoria, 1970). According to the 30th Annual Report of the Association on Formal and Social Hygiene in India found in a Nagpur Survey (1960) among 100 prostitutes, destitution, unemployment and lack of means of livelihood accounted for 36 per cent. In a Bombay Survey (Punekar, 1962) it was found that 72 per cent of the women entered this profession due to poverty. Davis, Kingsley (1971) also hold that the major cause of prostitution is economic.

(2) **Religious customs:** Some of the religious customs, which are though tabooed by law, encouraged the evil to flourish, the important being the practice of dedicating dancing girls to the temples. Girls once dedicated to the temples had to live a life of immorality, as it was enjoined upon by religion.

(3) **Social customs:** There are so many social customs such as:

   (a) the dowry system, still flourishing which sometimes makes it obligatory on young girls to remain spinsters till old age.

   (b) the child marriage which enforces young widows to live a life of chastity; finding it hard they face a prey to seductions either by the member of the family or the outsider.

   (c) the caste rigidity and custom of bride price equally nefarious in encouraging the people.

(d) the decay and gradual disappearance of the joint family system which offers little protection to widows and girls, who frequently enter this profession.

(e) the system of polygamy among Hindus and Muslims which results often in jealousy and marital unhappiness, and which makes the younger or the older co-wife seek her gratification outside the wed-lock.

(f) The social custom known as 'Reet' in the Himalayan region, whereby a man, who wants a new wife, sells off the former one and buys a new one.

(g) a custom among certain Bengali communities whereby widows are taken to the Vishwanath temple in Banaras and left there to spend the rest of their life in Bhagwat Bhajan. But most of them find themselves in the brothels of Banaras.

(h) a custom, among many communities, according to which the feudal lord or the spiritual guru has a right to spend with the young bride the first night after her marriage to one of his subjects or the devotees. Such ladies, after the death of her protector, slip into promiscuity with the neighbour or some outside element and soon court degradation.

(4) Social conditions: Sociological conditions are also responsible for prostitution. Due to rapid industrialization, fast urbanization, there is an acute shortage of living and housing accommodation. Memoria (1970) reports that 89 per cent of the total population of Bombay live in one room; similarly 62.5 per cent in Kanpur, 6 per cent in Nagpur, Gondia and Jabbalpur, 63 per cent in Madras and 73 per cent in Ahmedabad live in one room whereas 6 per cent in London, 5 per cent in Edinburg, 9 per cent in Dundee, and 13 per cent in Glasgow. So when the workers migrate from rural areas to work-centres, they cannot bring their wives, and they usually visit the red light area. Thus prostitution flourishes in industrial areas, mining areas and busties.

Ill-treatment to the daughter-in-law by the mother-in-law, sister-in-law and even by the husband is responsible for suicide or running away from the house; they fall an easy prey to anti-social elements. Kidnapping or seduction of young girls is also responsible for this vice. Early employment is an important factor in bringing the young girls into contact with immoral influences at an age when they are not equipped to make their own definitions and decisions and often fall prey to the advances of unscrupulous persons both within and without the household in which they work. They are merely anxious to improve their socio-economic status by the only means at hand and become prostitutes. Bad companies and recreational factors such as drinking, gambling, dance-halls, cafes, sexy films are also responsible for that. Generally, unsatisfactory home conditions, broken homes, immoral character of either parents, lack of understanding, sympathy and affection from the parents, during childhood and adolescence and lack of discipline, marital conflicts, and maladjustments are the causes of prostitution. Besides these factors, physical deformities, feeblemindedness, poverty, vested interests are the factors which lead a girl to become a prostitute.

On the basis of above review of literature it is assumed that the organized and disorganized (alcoholic, beggars, criminals and prostitutes) will differ in personality dimensions, for example frustration, anxiety, hostility and extroversion-neuroticism.

Therefore, the following general hypotheses were framed:

(1) There will be significant difference in frustration of organized (control) and disorganized (experimental

groups.

(2) There will be significant difference in anxiety of organized (control) and disorganized (experimental) groups.

(3) There will be significant difference in hostility of organized (control) and disorganized (experimental) groups.

(4) There will be significant difference in extroversion-neuroticism of organized (control) and disorganized (experimental) groups.

More specifically the following hypotheses were framed for verification:

(a) There will be significant difference in the mean regression-frustration score of disorganized groups (alcoholics, beggars, criminals and prostitutes) and normal persons.

(b) There will be significant difference in the mean fixation-frustration score of disorganized groups (alcoholics, beggars, criminals and prostitutes) and normal persons.

(c) There will be significant difference in the mean resignation-frustration score of disorganized groups (alcoholics, beggars, criminals and prostitutes) and normal persons.

(d) There will be significant difference in the mean aggression-frustration score of disorganized groups (alcoholics, beggars, criminals and prostitutes) and normal persons.

(e) There will be significant difference in the mean anxiety score of disorganized groups (alcoholics, beggars, criminals and prostitutes) and normal persons.

(f) There will be significant difference in the mean hostility score of disorganized groups (alcoholics, beggars, criminals and prostitutes) and normal persons.

(g) There will be significant difference in the mean extroversion score of disorganized groups (alcoholics, beggars, criminals and prostitutes) and normal persons.
(h) There will be significant difference in the mean neuroticism score of disorganized groups (alcoholics, beggars, criminals and prostitutes) and normal persons.

II
Methodology

Sample

After proper formulation of the hypothesis and defining the various terms used in the present study, the next step was to evolve a scientific methodology suitable for it. It will be recalled that the purpose of the present study was to investigate the difference between the organized and disorganized personalities and was confined to only four disorganized samples—Alcoholics, Beggars, Criminal and Prostitutes.

To have homogenous and unbiased sample, the subjects were matched for their age, sex, size of the family, residence, religion and culture. Age, sex, size of the family, residence, religion and culture have been shown to have important bearing on personality dimensions like extroversion, neuroticism, anxiety, frustration and hostility. It was gathered from the review of literature that extroversion, neuroticism, frustration and hostility are very much influenced by the age of the subject. As age increases aggression also increases (Govdanoughs, 1931; Pearde & Dahms, 1957). Satyarthi (1977) observed that age is significantly related to anxious attitude of students of both the sexes. Seemannova (1971) found that as the age increases anxiety decreases in the males but in the females at the age of 13-15 years old, their social anxieties differ. On the other hand Dutt (1968) and Jawa (1973) have found no relationship between anxiety and age. Age difference is also related with extroversion. Vidhu (1968) reported that extroversion is negatively related to age. But Singh (1968) found no significant age difference in extroversion. Dillubergerova (1969) has concluded that increasing age tended to elevate scores on extroversion. Eysenck (1969) reported that in both sexes the young have elevated E score. Pelka and Slugocki (1976) have reported that crime in women depends on both types of offences and age of the offender. Rao and Singh (1981) found that income and age, both, had a pronounced effect on the direction of aggression. Ranchfleisch (1981) reports that different age group did vary in their reactions. Lynch and Arudt (1973) found subjects making greater use of intropunitive responses with increasing age. Pareek (1964) reports that extrapunitiveness predominates at all age levels between age group of 4 to 13 years. He found that there is a definite tiend in its decline with increasing age. The form and intensity of aggressive reactions to frustrations vary with the child's age. Sears (1957) described the infant's response to a thwarting as a diffused rage. Only with maturation and learning does the hostility become focused into aggressive behaviour.

So far as sex is concerned, girls are more anxious as compared to the boys (Barton, 1971; Cowen *et al.,* 1965; Devi, 1969; Patjas, 1968; Penny, 1965; Satyarthi, 1977). But Singh and Nigam (1973) and Vangham and Taylor (1966) hold that males are more anxious than the females. Krishna (1971) finds a significant difference between males and females on their anxiety level. But Sinha (1975) observed that there was no sex difference on the anxiety level. Kishore and Pandey (1980) observed that neither sex nor interaction of sex and anxiety had any significant relationship with tolerance of ambiguous situation. In the field of extroversion and neuroticism it is reported (Eysenck & Eysenck, 1969; Kanekar & Mukherjee, 1972; Singh, 1968) that males are more extroverted than females. But Lai (1969) reported that girls were more extroverted than boys. Also Edwards *et al.* (1977) and Cloninger *et al.* (1978) observed sex difference in anti-social personality and crime. Further, it is found that females scored lower on the MAS than males (Svahum, Levitt & McAdeo, 1982). So far as the hostility and aggression are concerned, French and Bryce (1978) said that females are more aggressive than males. Sutton and Carlson (1977) also observed that females were significantly less punitive than males and significantly more committed to the ethic of personal conscience, than males. But Frodi (1978) found no sex difference in aggressive behaviour. Taylor and Duthie (1980) said that males are more aggressive than females. Maier (1949); Lansky, Crandall, Kagan and Barker (1961) confirm the fact that women are less aggressive.

Generally family size seems to affect girls much more than it does boys. Mayer (1947) made an experimental study to see the relationship between assertive behaviour of children and the behaviour of their parents. His findings suggest that aggressiveness is an outgrowth of the pattern of parent-child relations. And this pattern of parent-child relation depends on the size of the family members. Berkowitz (1962) cited the results of some studies made on the relationship between the aggressive behaviour of children and the affectionate attitude of their parents. And as the size of family increases, anxiety, depression, tension increases and the affectionate behaviour reduces. The college students, offsprings of cold mothers, generally showed a relatively high frequency of aggressive responses on the Rosenzweig P.F. test (Boruston & Coleman, 1956).

Social scientists generally agree that a family's position in the social satisfaction system has a considerable effect on the behaviour patterns, personality, frustration and anxiety. Winsox and Brainerd (1950) studied the aggressiveness of Negroes and Whites of South in U.S.A. on Rosenzweing P.F. Study. They found that Negroes tend to show more outward aggressiveness than Whites. McKee and Leader (1955) have reported that working-class pre-schoolers displayed more aggression in an experimental play situation than did their middle class peers. But Sears *et al.* (1957) did not find any difference between the aggressive behaviour of children of working class and middle class.

The social milieu is a significant source of frustration. Society sets up norms and rules, tacit conventions and prejudices that prevent the satisfaction of the individual needs. It sets up, e.g. an economic system, requiring that men satisfy essential needs through money and then makes the acquisition of money a difficult act. It sets up social, caste and class system preventing free social locomotion, so that a member of one caste or class may be thwarted in his desire to become a member of another and to acquire the privileges of the caste. Homey (1945) emphasizes the significance of social milieu in frustration causing neurosis. McCord, McCord and Howard (1961) have confirmed the views of neo-Freudians in their study on "familial correlates of aggression in non-delinquent male children." They report that aggressive reaction is the outcome of social environment. Berkowitz (1962) holds that lower economic status is one of the varieties of aversive conditions which can give rise to aggression.

In view of the above, the following criteria were fixed for selecting the sample:

1. Sex - Male
2. Age - 30 to 50 years
3. Religion and culture - Hindu
4. Size of the family - Average 6 to 10 persons
5. Economic status - Lower economic status (Rs. 100 to Rs. 500 per month)

Keeping in view the above criteria the following sample was selected for the present study.

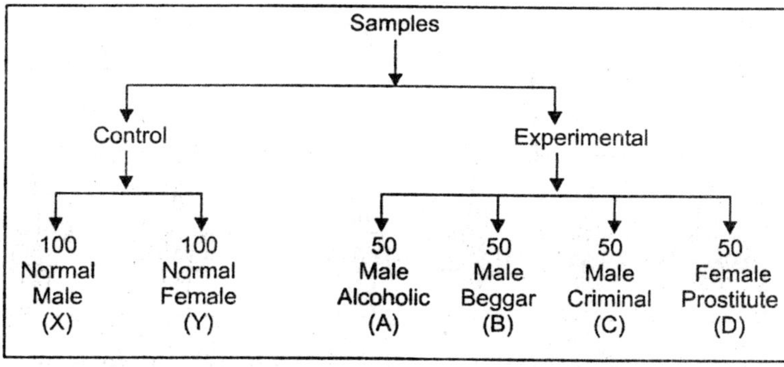

Tests used—The following four tests and inventories were used in the present study:

(1) Frustration test (Chauhan and Tiwari, 1972)
(2) Sinha W-A Self-Analysis Form (Anxiety Scale, 1968)
(3) Buss-Durkee Hostility Inventory (Hindi version rendered by Kafiluddin, 1977)
(4) Eysenck Personality Inventory (Akhtar, 1970)

A brief description of each of the tests is as follows:

(1) Frustration Test

This test has been developed by Chauhan and Tiwari (1972). The questionnaire method to study frustration was started long before (Dollard, 1944; Shaffer, 1947). The present test is in line with this and makes use of four categories, viz. regression, fixation, resignation and aggression consisting of ten items of each of the four modes of frustration. Thus the scale consists of 40 items. It studies effects of frustration upon the quality of a person's behaviour as a whole.

All the 40 items of the scale are presented in simple and brisk style. Each of the 40 items has five answers (multiple choice) graded on 5-point scale on the positive dimension and a Zero point on the negative dimension. Operationally defined, all the items of the scale are matters of behaviour in daily life. They are thus immensely meaningful and interesting. There is no obscurity or complexity in them.

Reliability of the Scale

The test re-test reliability for the scale on a sample of 55 adults with a test re-test gap of one month has been as under:

Frustration modes	*Reliability*
1. Regression	0.78
2. Fixation	0.92
3. Resignation	0.85
4. Aggression	0.87
5. As a whole	0.88

(2) Sinha W-A Self-Analysis Form (Anxiety Scale)

Sinha (1968) W-A Self-Analysis Form (Anxiety scale) was designed to measure anxiety. The form consists of 100 statements in Hindi dealing with different areas of anxiety. Against each statement 'Yes' and 'No' are printed. The subject has to encircle either of them to indicate his response. Each item which is checked 'Yes' is awarded the score of one. The score of every individual would be the total number of items checked positively. Thus the total scores which an individual can obtain range between 0 to 100. Higher scores indicate greater amount of anxiety in the subject.

The scale can be regarded as an extremely popular measure of individual's manifest anxiety and his drive level. Low score, i.e. below 25th percentile could be regarded as indicative of poor motivation and sluggishness. Very high scores, i.e. above the 75th percentile may be considered as symptomatic of such high state of anxiety which is likely to have a disruptive and interferring influence on the performance of a complex task. The middle group of scores would represent essentially 'normal' individual with moderately good drive level to stimulate performance without itself providing as interference (Sinha, 1968).

The scale constitutes a useful research tool. It gives a quick measure of anxiety for experimental and clinical and counselling purposes when the subject can only spare a short time. It is self-administrating and does not require the services of highly trained testers. It is eminently suitable for group administration as well as for individual testing. It is also useful instrument for locating the forms and dimensions in which anxiety may express itself. The test has no time limit but about half an hour (or preferably a full class hour) is enough for the administration of the test.

Items in the Sinha Anxiety Scale are classified into different forms and areas of anxiety. Firstly, items descriptive of physical manifestations like sweating, trembling, lack of sleep, indigestion, restlessness and other somatic reactions are put under the category of physical form (MPh). Other items referring to feelings, mental acts like worry, indecision, lack of confidence and the like are grouped under psychological manifestation (MPsy). There are nineteen items of MPh kind and eighty one of MPsy kind.

There are six areas of anxiety, viz. Health and Appearance (HA), General Worries (W), Guilt and Shame (GS), Social Relations (SR), Psychological Symptoms (SPsy) and Physical Symptoms (SPh). All the hundred items of the tests are classified into six areas of anxiety. Ten of them belong to the HA group, twenty four to W, eighteen to SR, ten to GS, twenty-three to SPsy, and fifteen to SPh.

Correlational and factorial study of the test (Sinha, 1965 a, b) has revealed that the two forms in which the anxiety manifests itself, viz., physical and psychological, are closely inter-related. The correlation between them is found to be (0.613) as also with the total test score (0.730 and 0.990). It indicates great communality of dimensions measured by the items pertaining to different forms of anxiety-manifestation.

Inter-correlations between six areas as also between each and total test score are high, the values ranging from 0.307 to 0.783 for the areas, and 0.711 to 0.880 between each area and the total test. They reveal a fairly high degree of generality between the areas.

The test possesses adequate reliability (Sinha, 1968) and has been shown to possess a good validity (Hundal, 1968; Sinha, 1963; Sinha, 1965). The split-half and test-retest reliabilities of the test have been found to be 0.92 and 0.85 respectively (Sinha, 1968). Standard error of measurement has been found to be 6.10 indicating that true score did not deviate too greatly from their true value.

Its relationship with a very commonly used measure of anxiety, viz. the Taylor's Manifest Anxiety Scale (Taylor, 1953) has been determined in a study by Sinha (1961, b). It has been found that the anxiety level and its distribution are similar in the two samples of Indian and American College population. The test correlates 0.73 with the Taylor's Manifest Anxiety Scale. The high correlation between the two is indicative of the communality of traits measured and of good validity. Hundal (1968) in his study on 200 male students of Panjab University has found score on the scale to correlate highly with those on other anxiety measures. Against Taylor's Scale, the correlation was 0.72, against Dutt's anxiety questionnaire (1964), it was 0.72 and against Cattell's PAT Anxiety Questionnaire (1957), it was 0.70. Sinha (1965a) claims that the test is a usual tool for assessing anxiety and it is efficacious in discriminating anxiety in normal and psychiatric cases. The high reliability and validity of the test and its standardization on an Indian sample prove it as quite fair and highly suitable for use in India as measure of drive level and anxiety.

(3) Buss-Durkee Hostility Inventory

Buss-Durkee Hostility Inventory (1957) has eight sub-scales consisting of 75 items, which measure different kinds of hostility and aggression, such as assault, indirect aggression, instability, negativism, resentment, guilt, suspicious and verbal aggression. The inventory provides separate score of different types of aggression as well as a composite score of aggression.

In this study a Hindi version of B.D.H. rendered by Kafiluddin (1977) was used. The Hindi version of this scale also consists of 75 items. Against each statement True and False categories of responses are given. Subjects are instructed to answer each item either as 'True' or 'False' whichever is applicable to them. A response of 'True' for every positive item is scored as 1 and similarly response of 'False' for every negative item is scored as 1. Range of possible scores on the inventory is from 0 to 75. The higher the test score the higher is the aggression in the subjects.

Buss and Durkee (1957) have reported a reliability co-efficient of 0.82 for full inventory, using test-retest method on a sample of 29 male-female college students. Kafiluddin (1977) has reported a reliability co-efficient of 81 for Hindi version of inventory using test-retest method on a sample of 50 male secondary school students. The reliability co-efficient of Hindi version is very close to the original inventory. Kafiluddin (1977) has also reported the internal consistency of this scale. The split-half reliability corrected by Spearmen Brown formula was 0.80 on a sample of 100 secondary school students. Pramanick (1980) had also determined the split-half reliability of the full scale using a sample of 50 males and females. The reliability co-efficient has been found to be 0.79 which is very close to the reliability co-efficient reported by Kafiluddin (1977).

(4) Eysenck Personality Inventory

Eysenck (1964) developed Eysenck Personality Inventory (E.P.I.), which supports to measure the two personality dimensions: (i) Extroversion-Introversion (E) and (ii) Neuroticism-Stability (N). The E.P.I. consists of two parallel forms–Form A and Form B. Form A comprises 57 questions, of these 24 questions are related to the E dimension, 24 to the N dimension and the rest 9 questions constitute the Lie Scale (L). Subjects proneness to desirability response set is identified through the L scale. In the present investigation, Form A has been used. Each question in the inventory has forced choice response alternatives of 'Yes' and 'No'. The subject has to encircle either of them to indicate his response. For every positive item related to either E, N or L dimension, a 'Yes' response is given a score of 1 and similarly for negative item, the 'No' response is scored as 1. Responses given otherwise are scored zero. High scores on either E, N scale indicate greater Extroversion Neuroticism respectively in the subject. Simply high score on the L scale shows that faked good is likely to have occurred. A score of 4 to 5 on the scale has been considered to constitute the cutting point where inventory answers ceased to be acceptable (Eysenck, 1964).

E.P.I. has been standardized on a large sample (12000) drawn from normal population of different professions, neurotics, psychotics, psychopaths and criminals differing widely in age, social class and education. The reliability score of this inventory has been recorded (Eysenck, 1964) by two methods—Test-retest and Split-half. The test-retest reliabilities for the E and N scales of Form A have been reported as 0.82 (N = 92) and 0.97 (N = 27); and 0.84 (N = 92) and 0.88 (N = 27) respectively. Similarly, the split-half reliability coefficients of Form A *vs*. Form B have been recorded to be 0.747 and 0.800 (N = 1655) for E and N scales respectively. Eysenck (1958b) had stated that theoretically the two dimensions were independent and consequently zero correlations would be expected between them, which means that the E and N scales are independent of each other for all practical purposes.

Evidence of construct validity exists in profusion in relation to MPI (Knapp, 1962) and by virtue of its close similarity to the EPI, this proof could also apply to the two scales in the EPI (Eysenck, 1964). In addition, direct evidence of validity of the inventory has been reported by Eysenck (1962) and Eysenck and Eysenck (1963). Using groups of extroverted and introverted subjects and stable and unstable subjects nominated by independent judges. They (Eysenck, 1962; Eysenck & Eysenck, 1963) have shown that there are clear and predictable differences in the EPI score of these groups. A Hindi version (Akhtar, 1970) of the EPI Form A was used to measure extroversion and neuroticism dimensions of personality of the subjects in the present study. Split-half and test-retest reliabilities of the scale employing normal subjects have been established by him. The split-half reliability coefficients of E and N scales were reported by Akhtar (1970) to be 0.757 and 0.703 respectively. Similarly, the test-retest reliability coefficients for the E and N scales were recorded to be 0.721 and 0.764 respectively. The correlation between the E and N scale scores of 10 students was found to be 0.043 for the Hindi version of the scale, confirming that E and N dimensions are independent of each other (Akhtar, 1970).

Procedure

It will be recalled that there were four samples on which this study was conducted. First of all the researcher selected four types of samples from the universe. An effort was made to impress upon the subjects that co-operation and honesty on their part were essential to reveal a lot of important facts concerning their personality. It was also emphasised that there were no good or bad answers. The subjects were assured that the answers given by them would be held in strict confidence. In this way a good rapport was established with the subjects before administering a test. Thereafter, the tests were administered in the following:

(1) Frustration test,
(2) Sinha W-A Self-Analysis Form (Anxiety scale),
(3) Buss-Durkee Hostility Inventory,
(4) Eysenck Personality Inventory.

All tests and inventories were self-administering. The researcher read the instructions given on the cover page of the inventories or tests before the administration. There was no time limit for the test or inventories. Ordinarily, the subjects took 20 to 25 minutes to complete the frustration test, 60 minutes respond to the Anxiety test, about 30 minutes to complete the Hostility Inventory and 35 to 40 minutes to respond to the E.P.I. The testing programme consisted of four sessions for each subject. Only one test was administered in each session to a small group of 5 to 10 subjects. In-between the two sessions, a short interval was provided. This interval varied from one to three days. It was found that they, on the whole, took the tests sincerely and enthusiastically.

III
Results and Discussion

The main purpose of the present study, it will be recalled, was to make a comparative study of the personality factors (Frustration, Anxiety, Hostility and Extraversion-Neuroticism) of organized (normal) and disorganized (Alcoholics, Beggars, Criminals and Prostitutes) groups. It was assumed that the groups will differ on personality factors.

Frustration: Organized and Disorganized Groups

The first hypothesis tested was that there would be significant difference between the frustration scores of organized and disorganized groups. Frustration test (Chauhan & Tiwari, 1972) was administered to 100 Normal males (X) and 50 male Alcoholics (A). 50 male Beggars (B), 50 male Criminals (C), and also 100 Normal females (Y) and 50 female Prostitutes (D) who constituted the sample of this study. The frustration test yielded four categories of scores: Regression, Fixation, Resignation and Aggression. Results of comparison of organized and disorganized groups on the four categories of scores follows:

> *Regression, Fixation, Resignation and Aggression — Organized and Disorganized Groups (Alcoholics, Beggars, Criminals and Prostitutes).*

To compare the regression, fixation, resignation and aggression scores of organized and disorganized groups *t*-test was used and the results are summarized in Table 3.1 and Table 3.2.

From Table 3.1 it is obvious that mean regression score of Normal male sample is 27.958 ± 8.852; of Alcoholic sample is 34.888 ± 6.468; of Beggar sample is 23.188 ± 3.828 and that of Criminal sample is 39.748 ± 7.779. The difference between Normal male sample mean regression score and Alcoholic sample mean regression score is significant (t = 4.925, df = 148, P < 0.001). Similarly, Normal male sample mean regression score is significantly different from Beggar sample mean regression score (t = 4.966, df = 148, P < 0.001). Also the difference between Normal male sample mean regression score and criminal sample mean regression score is significant (t =8.576, df = 148, P < 0.001). On the basis of the above comparisons it was concluded that Beggars had the lowest mean regression score and Criminals the highest mean regression score, with the Alcoholic mean regression score falling in between the mean regression score of the Beggars and Criminals. But the mean regression score of Normal male sample is higher than the mean regression score of Beggar sample.

A look at Table 3.1 indicates that mean fixation score of Normal male sample is 22.818 ± 18.418; of Alcoholic sample is 27.388 ± 7.891; of Beggar sample is 34.528 ± 6.946 and that of Criminal sample is 25.188 ± 6.193. The difference between male Normal sample mean fixation score and Alcoholic sample mean fixation score is significant (t = 3.136, df = 148, P < 0.001). Similarly, the difference between Normal sample mean fixation score and Beggar sample mean fixation score is highly significant (t = 8.117, df = 148, P < 0.001). Also the difference between normal sample mean fixation score and criminal sample mean fixation score is significant (t = 2.458, df = 148, P < 0.05). Therefore, it was concluded that Alcoholics, Beggars and Criminals all had higher mean fixation score than the normal sample.

Table 3.1: Comparison of regression, fixation, resignation and aggression scores of organized and disorganized (Alcoholic, Beggar and Criminal) groups

Group	N	Comparison groups	df	Regression		Fixation		Resignation		Aggression	
				Mean (SD)	CR	Mean (SD)	CR	Mean (SD)	CR	Mean (SD)	CR
Normal Male (X)	100			27.958 (8.852)	—	22.813 (18.418)	—	28.658 (8.497)	—	26.448 (7.218)	—
Alcoholic Male (A)	50	X & A	148	34.888 (6.468)	4.925**	27.388 (7.891)	3.136**	26.288 (6.527)	1.874^{NS}	28.888 (7.486)	1.269^{NS}
Beggar Male (B)	50	X & B	148	23.188 (3.828)	4.966**	34.528 (6.946)	8.117**	22.868 (5.887)	4.944**	22.188 (3.772)	4.713**
Criminal Male (C)	50	X & C	148	39.748 (7.779)	8.576**	26.188 (6.193)	2.458*	27.548 (9.665)	8.883**	23.528 (8.286)	2.183*

*P 0.05 **P 0.001

Table 3.2: Comparison of regression, fixation, resignation and aggression scores of organized and disorganized (prostitute) groups

Group	N	df	Regression		Fixation		Resignation		Aggression	
			Mean (SD)	*CR*	*Mean (SD)*	*CR*	*Mean (SD)*	*CR*	*Mean (SD)*	*CR*
Normal Female (Y)	100	148	25,888 (6.947)	1.469^{NS}	25.580 (7.524)	5.890**	24.620 (9.263)	3.722**	29.800 (8.845)	1.132^{NS}
Prostitutes Female (D)	50		27.968 (7.068)		33.288 (5.208)		29.980 (3.977)		31.580 (6.549)	

**P<.001

A perusal of Table 3.1 also shows that mean resignation score of Normal male sample is 28.658 ± 8.497; of Alcoholic sample is 26.288 ± 6.527; of Beggar sample is 22.868 ± 5.887 and that of Criminal sample is 27.548 ± 9.655. The difference between male Normal sample mean resignation score and Alcoholic sample mean resignation score is not significant (t = 1.874, df = 148, P >0.05). The difference between normal sample mean resignation score and Beggar sample mean resignation score is significant (t = 4.944, df = 148, P < 0.01). Also the difference between Normal sample mean resignation score and Criminal sample mean resignation score is highly significant (t = 8.883, df = 148, P < 0.001). Thus on the basis of above comparisons, it was concluded that all the three disorganized groups (Alcoholics, Beggars and Criminals) had less mean resignation score than the normal. But Beggars had the lowest mean resignation score and Criminals had the highest mean resignation score, with the Alcoholic mean resignation score falling in between the mean resignation scores of Beggars and Criminals.

A glance at Table 3.1 further shows that mean aggression score of Normal sample is 26.448 ± 7.218; of Alcoholic sample is 28.888 ± 7.486; of Beggar sample is 22.188 ± 3.772 and that of Criminal sample is 23.528 ± 8.286. The difference between male normal sample mean aggression score and Alcoholic sample mean aggression score is not significant (t = 1.269; df = 148, P < 0.05). The difference between male Normal sample mean aggression score and Beggar sample mean aggression score is significant (t = 4.713, df = 148, P < 0.001). Also the difference between male Normal sample mean aggression score and Criminal sample mean aggression score is significant (t = 2.183, df = 148, P < 0.05). Therefore, it was concluded that Beggars had the lowest mean aggression score and Alcoholic the highest mean aggression score, with the Criminal mean aggression score falling in between the mean aggression scores of the Beggars and Alcoholics. The normal male sample mean aggression score stood in between the mean aggression scores of the Criminals and Alcoholics.

An inspection of Table 3.2 shows that mean regression score of Normal female sample is 25.888 ± 6.947 and that of Prostitute sample is 27.968 ± 7.068. The difference between Normal female sample mean regression score and Prostitute sample mean regression score is insignificant (t = 1.469, df ± 148, P < 0.05). On the basis of above comparison, it was concluded that Prostitutes had the higher mean regression score than the mean regression score of Normal female.

From Table 3.2 it is also apparent that mean fixation score of normal female sample is 25.580 ± 7.524 and that of Prostitute sample is 33.288 ± 5.208. The difference between normal female sample mean fixation score and Prostitute sample mean fixation score is significant (t = 5.870, df = 148, P < 0.001). Therefore, on the basis of above comparison it was concluded that Prostitutes had higher mean fixation score than the mean fixation score of normal females.

A look at Table 3.2 indicates that mean resignation score of normal female sample is 24.620 ± 9.263 and that of Prostitute sample is 29.980 ± 3.977. The difference between normal female sample mean resignation score and Prostitute sample mean resignation score is significant (t = 3.722, df = 148, P < 0.00l). Therefore, on the basis of above results it was concluded that prostitutes had the higher mean resignation score than the mean resignation score of normal females.

From Table 3.2 it is further evident that mean aggression score of Normal female sample is 29.800 ± 8.845 and that of Prostitute sample is 31.580 ± 6.549. The difference between Normal female sample mean aggression score and Prostitute sample mean aggression score is insignificant (t = 1.132, df = 148, P >0.05). On the basis of above comparison it was concluded that Prostitutes had higher mean aggression score than the mean aggression score of normal females.

The results of the comparisons made above may be summarised as follows:

1. The Alcoholics and Criminals had significantly higher mean regression score as compared to the normal male group.
2. The Beggars had significantly lower mean regression score as compared to the normal male group.
3. The Prostitutes had higher mean regression score as compared to the normal female group, but there was no significant difference.
4. The Alcoholics, Beggars and Criminals had significantly higher fixation score as compared to the normal male group.
5. The Prostitutes had higher mean fixation score as compared to the normal female group.
6. The Beggars and Criminals had significantly lower mean resignation score as compared to the normal male group. The Alcoholics had also lower mean resignation score as compared to the normal male group but the difference was not significant.
7. The Prostitutes had significantly higher mean resignation score as compared to the normal female group.
8. The Beggars and Criminals had significantly lower mean aggression score as compared to the normal male group.
9. The Alcoholics had higher mean aggression score as compared to the normal male group, but the differences were not significant.
10. The Prostitutes had higher mean aggression score as compared to the normal female group, but the difference was not significant.

Thus the results of the present study show that in all the modes of frustration, i.e. regression, fixation, resignation and aggression, the disorganized groups had higher mean score as compared to the organized group. The reason seems to that disorganized groups take to maladaptive modes of resolution of frustration and when achievement of a goal is blocked, they react in a maladaptive way. Frustration is closely related to the problem of adjustment, change, personality development or growth (Underwood, 1949). It has been noted earlier that if an anticipated desirable outcome is not attained, frustration occurs and this in turn has some observable effects on behaviour. In other words there must be blocking of goal directed activities as the antecedent condition and some behavioural event as the consequence. Two important antecedent events for frustration are barriers and deficiency. Barriers may be external physical objects or internal states, whereas a deficiency is a lack of the necessary ability in the individual to attain a goal. In all social strata and in all 'phases' of personality development, each one of us is bound to face, repeatedly the problem of frustration. As Lawson (1966) said that it is the root of all behaviour disorders. Murphy (1947) has pointed out the effects of frustration in moulding personality similar views have been expressed by Ruch (1958). According to him the person who is maladaptive, his reactions become disorganized and exaggerated (Ruch, 1958). It is well known that disorganized groups constitute a deprived and disadvantaged group. Through out their life history beggars have learnt to modify their needs and motives in response to an obstacle. Even though, they may feel that the other person or the social obstacles that are put in the way of satisfaction of their needs to be unjust they cannot express their anger or hostility for fear of risking social disapproval, physical violençe or other punishments. But the normal persons can afford to do so because they are placed better off in relation to the disorganized groups. Attack upon and the removal of the obstacle in their case is an accepted behaviour, but no so in the case of disorganized personality. As such a lower level of aggression among the Beggars and Criminals seems justified.

The Beggars are a pitiable lot in our society. Their ego is not strong; because whenever one wants to come out and assert his rights he is either punished or and discouragement come too often they weaken the ego of individual concerned. It is a common knowledge that individuals with weak ego are not in a position to attempt to remove or surmount obstacles coming in the way of need satisfaction. Consequently simple withdrawal or compromise or apathy results. They cannot revolt against the situation, they realize that they are not able-bodied persons. They have very little social prestige and position in the society. As the individual learns to associate certain objects and situations with frustration and hunt he avoids rather than attacks them. For prostitutes most of the situations cannot be dealt with successfully by either direct attack or withdrawal. Usually it becomes necessary to work out some sort of compromise which may mean accepting substitute goal or resorting to retreatism. For Alcoholics, Beggars, Criminals, and Prostitutes, who have been subjected to unrestricted isolation and lived under extreme conditions of continued frustration, loss of hope; becoming resigned and apathetic and adapting themselves to restricted way of living is but natural. Lack of love and continued neglect are fertile grounds for growth of beggary, vagrancy, prostitution, criminality, alcoholism etc. Choisy (1961), Macrov (1965), Tackman *et al.* (1967), Esselstyn (1968), Greenwald (1970), Devis (1971) and Gray (1973) all mention that unsatisfactory relationship with parents and consequent frustration as a fact of life for prostitutes.

As Faretra (1981) reports that familial background and social environment are also responsible for aggression and frustration and the socially disorganized persons are the product of bad family background and bad social environment. Hind-men (1977) asserts that child abuse and neglect are the cause of alcoholism. Because of this abuse and negligence, the child becomes frustrated and develops the habit of stealing (Moore, Chamberain and Mukal, (1979). Gnapp (1976) also confirms the result by saying that alcoholic and drug addicts are related to anxiety, depression and frustration. Feelings of dependence and need for love are basic emotions, when the demand for love is frustrated, aggressive behaviour does arise. These also take place in the case of prostitutes. Thus aggressive emotion is not an instinct but a product of a particular relationship to environment, especially to refusal and rejection by the mother. Studies by Weiss and Fine (1956) have shown that the aggressively anti-social persons emerged from an environment, characterized by parental rejection, familiar discord, punitive discipline and inconsistency. According to Berkowitz (1975) parents can affect child's likelihood of acting aggressively in a number of ways. Lack of parental love and protection increases the probability that the child will behave aggressively. In this connection, alcoholic intoxication has been noted for its inhibition releasing and judgement—altering effects—(Gudevich and Bourne, 1970). Its facilitating effect on violent behaviour is not in doubt (Guze *et al.*, 1962) at all.

Pestonjee and Bagchi (1979) report that persons with lower adjustments have higher aggression scores. In the present study out of the alcoholics, the beggars, the criminals and the prostitutes, most of them have displayed high aggression scores. While explaining this finding recourse seems lie in the frustration-aggression hypothesis.

Anxiety—Organized and Disorganized Groups

The second hypothesis tested was that there would be significant difference between the anxiety scores of organized and disorganized groups. Anxiety test (Sinha, 1968) was administered to 100 normal males (X) and 50 male Alcoholics (A); 50 male Beggars (B); 50 male Criminals (C) and also 100 normal females (Y) and 50 female Prostitutes (D) who constituted the sample of this study. Results of comparison of organized and disorganized groups are as follows:

To compare the anxiety scores of organized and disorganized groups (Alcoholics, Beggars, Criminals and Prostitutes) *t*-test was used and the results are summarized in Table 3.3 and Table 3.4.

Table 3.3: Comparison of Anxiety Scores of organized and disorganized (Alcoholic, Beggar and Criminal) groups

Groups	*N*	*Mean*	*SD*	*Comparison groups*	*t*	*df*	*P-Value*
Normal Male (X)	100	27.668	18.304	–	–	–	–
Alcoholics (A)	50	40.860	19.182	X and A	3.999	148	< 0.01
Beggars (B)	50	45.828	16.148	X and B	5.885	148	< 0.01
Criminals (C)	50	54.688	14.947	X and C	9.586	148	< 0.01

Table 3.4: Comparison of Anxiety Scores of organized and disorganized (Prostitutes) group

Groups	*N*	*Mean*	*SD*	*t*	*df*	*P-Value*
Normal Female (Y)	100	44.100	20.552	7.606	148	< 0.01
Prostitutes (D)	50	69.680	11.481			

From Table 3.3 it is clear that mean anxiety score of normal male sample is 27.668 ± 18.304; of Alcoholic sample is 40.860 ± 9.182; of Beggar sample is 45.828 ± 16.148 and that of Criminal sample is 54.688 ± 14.947. The difference between Normal male sample mean anxiety score and Alcoholic sample mean anxiety score is significant (t = 3.999, df = 148, P < 0.01). Similarly, Normal male sample mean anxiety score is significantly different from Beggar sample mean anxiety score (t = 5.885, df = 148, P < 0.001). Also the difference between Normal male sample mean anxiety score and Criminal sample mean anxiety score is significant (t = 9.586, df = 148, P < 0.001). On the basis of above comparisons it was concluded that in the disorganized groups Criminals had the highest mean anxiety score and Alcoholics the lowest mean anxiety score, with the Beggars mean anxiety score falling in-between the mean anxiety score of the Criminals and Alcoholics. Also the normal male group had the lowest mean anxiety score as compared to the disorganized groups.

A glance at Table 3.4 shows that mean anxiety score of Normal female sample is 44.100+20.552 and that of Prostitute sample is 69.680±11.481. The difference between Normal female sample mean anxiety score and Prostitute sample mean anxiety score is highly significant (t = 7.606, df = 148, P < 0.001). Therefore, on the basis of above results it was concluded that Prostitutes were significantly more anxious than the Normal female group.

The results of the comparisons made above may be summarized as follows:

1. Alcoholics, Beggars and Criminals had significantly higher anxiety score as compared to the Normal male group.
2. Prostitutes had significantly higher anxiety score as compared to the Normal female group.
3. Of the four disorganized groups—Alcoholics, Beggars, Criminals and Prostitutes, the Prostitutes were the most anxious group.

Now let us try to give reasons as to why disorganized groups suffered more anxiety than the organized groups. It is well known that alcohol reduces anxiety and it is easy to envisage highly anxious people turning to alcohol to reduce their anxiety and the drinking habit becoming reinforced by drive reduction. About Alcoholism the psychoanalytic approach emphasizes the importance of oral fixation. Based on a longitudinal study of high school students followed through college, Jessor and Jessor (1977) proposed that adolescent deviant behaviour is determined by a multivariate netwotk of personality and environmental factors. The alcoholic symtomatology was described as a neurotic pattern of self-centredness, immaturity, dependence, resentfulness and the irresponsibility associated with inability to face reality. The present result is also in line with the result of Mendelson *et al.* (1964) and McNamee *et al.* (1968) who report that there was positive relationship between alcohol consumption and anxiety.

So far the beggars are concerned they also have been found to be significantly more anxious than the normals. They suffer from inferiority complex. They consider themselves as out-castes, unacceptable by society. They realise that they have very little social prestige and position in society. They also often experience special kind of alienation and social distance from conventional society. Beggars are also fearful of the society and this fear of ridicule and neglect results in the development of anxiety which becomes part of their personality. This reasoning also confirms the results of Sarason and Spielberger (1975) that more educated prestigious and high income groups are less anxious and *vice versa*. A plausible hypothesis is that those who say that they are dissatisfied because they need more money are experiencing more severe economic pressure and would, therefore, be more anxious than those who think that they are worth more pay.

Eysenck (1958) has reported that "neuroticism refers to the general emotional liability of a person, his emotional over-responsiveness and his liability to neurotic breakdown under stress." Psychologically speaking, in neuroticism, the individual is overwhelmed with a particular type of conflict which generates anxiety. Also anxiety is considered as one of the important constituents of neuroticism. The vast majority of crimes and delinquencies are impulsive acts or efforts to achieve financial gain, personal status, or some similar objective. Such people are conscious of their wrong doing which ordinarily is accompanied by some degree of anxiety and feelings of guilt. Argyle's (1964) observation that delinquents have weak guilt feeling is controversial, because Persons (1970b) found that guilt was negatively correlated with number of criminal offenses. Giannell

(1970) also reported that criminals were lower on internal inhibition than non-criminals, especially on guilt feeling. Similar findings were reported by McQuaid (1970).

The other view point leaves heavily on psychoanalytic concept and postulates that guilt generates tension, conflict and anxiety in the individual. Zulliger (1956) opines that delinquencies are usually related to the total personality of the delinquents and to the milieu in which they have been raised. The offender who feels guilty often finds escape from his conflicts of conscience through sharing his guilt by formation of gangs. Baugh and Carpenter (1962) argue that delinquents, because of their warped ego and retarted personality development, must discharge tension upon the environment in an aggressive and over compensatory manner. This behaviour pattern, however, leads to internal guilt feelings and intro-punitive drives. There is a good deal of evidence that criminals tend to have high levels of anxiety. The earlier literature pointing to this conclusion was reviewed by Eysenck (1964). This has subsequently been confirmed in several studies in which questionnaires of anxiety or neuroticism have been given to criminals (Eysenck and Eysenck, 1964; Burgess, 1972 a, b; Iwawaki, Sujiyama & Nauri, 1964; Cattell, Eber & Tatsuoka, 1970; Pierson & Kelly, 1963; Warburton, 1965; Houghngi & Forrest, 1970; and Little, 1963). A high crime rate is, therefore, taken as a positive index of national anxiety levels. Also more educated and more prestigious people are less anxious (Sarason & Spielberger, 1975). Thus it is proved that a criminal is tormented by an excessive feeling of guilt and his criminal acts are aimed at reducing it. And if criminals suffer with guilt feelings, naturally they should be higher on anxiety than the normals, and the present finding is thus confirmed.

The U.N. Committee's (1959) observations also indicate that 'prostitutes have generally slight mental and psychical abnormalities—emotional instability, abnormal lack of emotion, pronounced nervousness or anxiety and so on and that a considerable number of them suffer from a psychosexual immaturity, very often caused by early childhood frustrations.' Ardu (1892) author of Lambrosian school published his result of observations as to the frequency of abnormalities among prostitutes. Anxiety is one of the abnormalities, so it confirmed the present result. Rolph (1955) said that prostitutes are influenced by psychopathological factors. Due to unfulfilled emotional and social needs they generally either abstain from making social contacts or fail to do so. This is owing to many factors including considering themselves as outcaste, unacceptable by society. They often experience a special kind of alienation and social distance from conventional society. Most of the girls disclosed feelings of loneliness and that they were prepared to do anything to overcome it (Kapur, 1978). As Carellia (1906) said that prostitutes tend to form a class showing morphological inferiority to normal women. So they usually avoid contact with so-called respectable people. Quite closed to outside society, these girls live in a 'world of their own'. Their interaction is mostly with their client. Like other forms of deviance, the life of prostitution "commits a person at the most deeply experienced levels of the self, and in the process produces far greater similarities between prostitutes than could be expected on the basis of any set of etiological characteristic" (Sills, 1968).

Since they are isolated from primary relationships they feel, and are, alienated and alone and thus need emotionally meaningful social relationships. But as seen through their life-histories these girls have such poor opinion of themselves and an inner feeling of worthlessness because of their parents' rejection that it becomes very difficult for them to achieve any kind of satisfactory relationship with other people. In other words they are almost incapable of forming and establishing close, meaningful and mature interpersonal relationships (Benjamin, 1951; Glover, 1953: Benjamin & Ellish, 1955; Rolph, 1955; Greenwald, 1958).

The very high incidence of alcoholism among call girls also indicates their insecurity, anxiety and general failure to adjust to the world (Kapur, 1978). Borelli and Starck (1957), Benjamin and Masters (1966), Kemp (1970) found that prostitutes were emotionally unstable and maladjusted personalities. Kapur (1978) also holds that prostitutes drank to overcome their frustrations, fears, anxieties, inhibitions, embarrassments and complexes including the guilt complex. All these show that prostitutes are greatly frustrated and highly anxious persons. In the present study also it will be remembered the prostitutes have high anxiety score than the normals.

Hostility (BDH): Organized and Disorganized Groups

The third hypothesis tested was that there would be significant difference between the hostility scores of organized and disorganized groups BDH test (Kafiluddin, 1977) was administered to 100 normal males (X) and 50 male Alcoholics (A), 50 male Beggars (B), 50 male Criminals (C), and 100 normal females (Y) and 50 female Prostitutes (D) who constituted the sample of this study. Results of organized and disorganized groups are as follows:

To compare the hostility scores of organized and disorganized (Alcoholics, Beggars, Criminals and Prostitutes) groups, r-test was used and the results are stated in Table 3.5 and Table 3.6.

Table 3.5: Comparison of Hostility scores of organized and disorganized (Alcoholic, Beggar and Criminal) groups

Groups	*N*	*Mean*	*SD*	*Comparison groups*	*t*	*df*	*P-Value*
Normal Male (X)	100	36.858	7.415	–	–	–	–
Alcoholics (A)	50	42.720	10.329	X and A	4.034	148	< 0.01
Beggars (B)	50	41.778	10.822	X and B	2.87	148	< 0.01
Criminals (C)	50	47.248	12.414	X and C	5.817	148	< 0.01

From an inspection of Table 3.5 it is obvious that mean hostility score of Normal male sample is 36.858 ± 7.415; of

Table 3.6: Comparison of Hostility Scores of organized and disorganized (Prostitutes) group

Groups	*N*	*Mean*	*SD*	*t*	*df*	*P-Value*
Normal Female (Y)	100	40.320	8.088	5.151	148	< 0.01
Prostitutes (D)	50	8.120	6.849			

Alcoholic sample is 42.720 ± 10.329; of Beggar sample is 41.778 ± 10.822 and that of Criminal sample is 47.248. The difference between Normal male sample mean hostility score and Alcoholic sample mean hostility score is significant (t = 4.034, df = 148, P < 0.001). Similarly, Normal male sample mean hostility score is significantly different from Beggar sample mean hostility score (t = 2.87, df = 148, P < 0.001). Also the difference between Normal male sample mean hostility score and Criminal sample mean hostility score is significant (t = 5.817, df = 148, P < 0.001). On the basis of the above comparisons it was concluded that all the disorganized groups had significantly higher hostility score than the normal male group. Among disorganized groups, criminals had the highest mean hostility score and Beggars the lowest mean hostility score, with the Alcoholic mean hostility score falling in between the mean hostility score of the Criminals and Beggars.

From Table 3.6 it is also apparent that mean hostility score of Normal female sample is 40.320 ± 8.088 and that of Prostitute sample is 48.120 ± 6.849. The difference between Normal female sample mean hostility score and Prostitute sample mean hostility score is significant (t = 5.151, df = 148, P < 0.001). Therefore, it was concluded that Prostitutes were significantly more hostile than the normal female sample.

The results of the comparisons made above may be summarized as follows:

1. Alcoholics, Beggars and Criminals had significantly higher hostility score as compared to the Normal male group.
2. Prostitutes had significantly higher hostility score as compared to the Normal female group.
3. Prostitutes constituted the most hostile group among the disorganized groups, viz. Alcoholics, Beggars, and Criminals.

Alcoholic intoxication has been noted for its "inhibition-releasing and judgement altering effects" (Gulevich and Bourne, 1970). Its facilitating effect on violent behaviour has never been in doubt (Guze, Tuason, Gatfield, Stewart, and Picken, 1962; Wolfgang and Strohm, 1956). Much violence, criminal homicide in particular, is committed in a state of alcoholic intoxication. Taylor, Schmutte and Leonard (1977) hold physical aggression as a function of alcohol and frustration. The further report that the persons who were intoxicated, were more aggressive than the persons who were non-intoxicated. In the present study also it was found that Alcoholics were significantly more hostile than the normals.

As we know beggars are a deprived and despised group. Although they are deprived but they are ambitious also. And when the ambitions are not fulfilled, they become frustrated and it is well known that frustration instigates behaviour that may be hostile or aggressive. Zillman (1979) maintains that frustration is not a sufficient, but a necessary, condition for hostility and aggression. However, there is considerable evidence supporting the view that frustration becomes a potent inducer of aggression when it is associated with personal attack. In a number of investigations it has been shown that frustration produces hostility or aggression more readily when it is perceived as arbitrary, unjustified, intentional, or unmitigated rather than accidental or warranted (Burnstein and Worchel, 1962; Cohen, 1955;

Kregarmen and Woichel, 1961; Mallick and McCandles, 1966; Pastore, 1952; Rotbams and Worchel, 1960; Zillmann, Bryant, Cantor and Day, 1975; Zillmann and Cantor, 1976 b). These investigations generally corroborate Buss's (1961, 1971) contention.

In the present investigation it was found that beggars suffer with high anxiety in comparison of normals. Singh (1976) found a closer relationship between hostility and anxiety. Therefore, it seems plausible to assume that, where there is some sort of anxiety—implicit or explicit, the tension created by this anxiety is reduced or eliminated through the aggressive behaviour. Hence, those who are generally anxiety ridden, for them aggressive behaviour becomes a tension reductive process. The more deprived and frustrated persons are they tend to be more outwardly aggressive. And this exactly explains why the beggars are more aggressive.

Crimes against property, which are incentive motivated by definition, can be seen as hostile activities that only in the exception entail aggressive behaviour. The analysis of violent crimes, especially criminal homicide, makes it abundantly clear that aggressive actions that inflict severe consequences upon the victim are primarily motivated by annoyance (Mulvihill, Tumin, & Curtis, 1969). The results of the present study are in line with the findings of Kundu and Mukherjee, 1958; Washburn, 1963; Cole, Fisher, and Cole, 1968). But there are other studies (Giannell, 1966a; Blackburn, 1968; Silber & Courtless, 1968; Jamuar, 1981), which are report that criminals are higher on hostility than non-criminals. It has been argued (Berkowitz, 1962) that criminal behaviour and aggression are interlinked with each other. Criminals, therefore, should invariably possess high hostility. The frustration-aggression hypothesis states that frustration which results from the blockage of goal directed activity leads to aggression. Criminals have experienced punitive discipline (Sollenberger, 1968) during childhood which generated frustration and consequently aggression. Later on retribution from society further aggravates the feeling of frustration leading to more hostile feeling. Criminals have not only been deprived of parental attention and recognition by society (Kundu & Mukherjee, 1958) but also have experienced economic deprivation (Wood, 1961) and status deprivation (Cohen, 1955). These deprivations lead to further frustration and hence more aggression. It is natural, therefore, that criminals should have greater amount of hostility than the normals. Thus our results are supported by above findings.

Prostitutes' strong anti-masculine attitude Chesser (1958) and hostility towards men Greenald (1970) are well recognised. It is because, as Chesser (1958) opined, the prostitutes cannot possibly love the number of men passing in and out of their business life, and so, in sheer self-defence, keep themselves emotionally detached from the transitory relationships with clients by over-emphasising their hate towards the clients and men in general. Or it may be that since the prostitutes know consciously or even unconsciously the attitude of society, in fact, mainly of men towards them is of contempt, as a reaction of which they start developing their attitude of contempt towards them (Chesser, 1971).

As seen in the life histories and reports of a large number of call girls, they generally suffer from feelings that they had been deprived, disapproved, and damaged by the family and society, and the resultant desire to retaliate tends to make them reject the values of the society and is liable to make them rebellious, defy authority and to indulge in social, anti-social and sexually deviant behaviour. And because they could not or do not adhere to the values and norms of the society, they develop guilt feelings and these are the reasons, due to which prostitutes are more hostile among the disorganized groups. The hostility and the revenge motive that these girls harbour for the family and society when turned towards their own selves, manifests itself in their masochistic and even suicidal tendencies by way of degrading and debasing themselves, and when turned towards others it manifests itself in sadistic tendencies by way of deriving pleasure in torturing the mother or father or father substitutemen—through their sexually deviant and socially disapproved acts. Abraham (1953) sees prostitution as an act of hostility directed against the father. Kapur (1978) also refers to guilt feelings and hostility towards men among prostitutes. Thus the findings of the present research, that the prostitutes have significantly higher hostility scores than the normals may be explained on the lines of the above reasoning.

Due to intoxication, deprivation, frustration, dissatisfaction, unjustification, etc. the disorganized groups were more hostile than the normal groups. In the present investigation it was also found that of all the disorganized groups, the prostitutes were the most hostile group, the reason behind it seems to be their insecurity, disapproval by the society, lack of sympathy and hate which has permeated their life.

EPI—Organized and Disorganized Groups

The fourth hypothesis tested was that there would be significant difference between the EPI scores of organized and disorganized groups. EPI (Akhtar, 1970) was administered to 100 normal males (X) with 50 male Alcoholics (A), 50 male Beggars (B), 50 male Criminals (C) and also 100 normal females (Y) with 50 female Prostitutes (D), who constituted the sample of this study. Eysenck Personality Inventory (Akhtar, 1970) yielded two categories of scores: Extroversion and Neuroticism. Results of comparison of organized and disorganized groups on the two categories of scores follows:

Extroversion Neuroticism—Organized and Disorganized Groups (Alcoholics, Beggars, Criminals and Prostitutes):

To compare the Extroversion scores of organized and disorganized groups, *t*-test was used and the results are computed in Table 3.7 and Table 3.8.

It is apparent from Table 3.7 that mean Extroversion score of Normal male sample is 11.888 ± 3.381; of Alcoholic sample is 14.259 ± 3.961; of Beggar sample is 8.280 ± 2.276 and that of Criminal sample is 15.131 ± 4.613. The difference between Normal male sample mean extroversion score and Alcoholic sample mean extroversion score is significant (t = 3.625, df = 148, P < 0.00l). Similarly, Normal male sample mean extroversion score is significantly different from Beggar sample mean extroversion score (t = 7.742. df = 148, P < 0.001). Also the difference between Normal male sample mean extroversion score and Criminal sample mean extroversion score is significant (t = 4.418, df = 148, P < 0.001). On the basis of the above findings it was concluded that Beggars had lower extroversion score than the Normal male sample. But Alcoholics and Criminals bad greater extroversion score than the Normal male sample. In other words Alcoholics and Criminals are extroverted and Beggars are neither extroverted nor neurotic.

Table 3.7: Comparison of Extroversion-Neuroticism scores of organized and disorganized (Alcoholic, Beggar and Criminal) groups

Group	*N*	*Comparison groups*	*df*	*Extroversion*		*Neuroticism*	
				Mean (SD)	*CR*	*Mean (SD)*	*CR*
Normal Male (X)	100	—		11.888 (3.381)	—	9.991 (4.351)	
Alcoholic Male (A)	50	X and A	148	14.259 (3.961)	3.625**	13.171 (4.847)	3.92**
Beggar Male (B)	50	X and B	148	8.280 (2.276)	7.742**	5.428 (2.255)	8.481**
Criminal Male (C)	50	X and C	148	15.131 (4.613)	4.418**	16.013 (5.316)	6.945**

**P<.001

A glance at Table 3.7 shows that mean Neuroticism score of Normal male sample is 9.991 ± 4.351; of Alcoholic sample is 13.171 ± 4.847; of Beggar sample is 5.428 ± 2.255 and that of

Table 3.8: Comparison of Extroversion-Neuroticism scores of organized and disorganized (prostitute) groups

Group	*N*	*df*	*Extroversion*		*Neuroticism*	
			Mean (SD)	*CR*	*Mean (SD)*	*CR*
Normal Female (Y)	100	148	10.331 (2.932)	5.551**	11.010 (4.301)	4.752 **
Prostitutes Female (D)	50		13.251 (3.101)		13.800 (2.840)	

**P<.001

Criminal sample is 16.013 ± 5.316. The difference between Normal male sample mean neuroticism score and Alcoholic sample mean neuroticism score is significant (*t* – 3.92, df – 143, P < 0.001). Similarly, the difference between Normal male sample mean neuroticism score and Beggar sample mean neuroticism score is significant (*t* = 8.481, df = 148, P < 0.001). Also the difference between Normal male sample mean neuroticism score and Criminal sample mean neuroticism score is significant (*t* = 6.945, df = 148, P < 0.001). Thus on the basis of the above results it is concluded that in comparison to the Normal persons Alcoholics and Criminals are more neurotic. Among the disorganized groups, Beggars had the lowest mean neuroticism score and Criminal had the highest mean neuroticism score, with the Alcoholic mean neuroticism score falling in between the two sample mean neuroticism score of Beggars and Criminals.

A perusal of Table 3.8 shows that mean extroversion score of Normal female sample is 10.331 ± 2.932 and that of Prostitutes is 13.251 ± 3.101. The difference between Normal female sample mean extroversion score and Prostitute sample mean extroversion score is significant (*t* = 5.551, df = 148, P < 0.001). Therefore, it was concluded that the mean extroversion score of Prostitutes were much more high in comparison of Normal female sample.

An inspection of Table 3.8 also shows that mean neuroticism score of Normal female sample is 11.010 ± 4.301 and that of Prostitutes is 13.800 ± 2.840. The difference between Normal female sample mean neuroticism score and Prostitutes sample mean neuroticism score is significant (t = 4.752, df = 148, P < 0.001). Thus it was concluded that the mean neuroticism score of Prostitutes were greater than the Normal female sample.

The results of the comparison made above may be summarized as follows:

1. Alcoholics were significantly more extroverted and more neurotic than the Normal male group.
2. Beggars were significantly less extrovert and less neurotic than the normal male group.
3. Criminals were significantly more extroverted and more neuroric than the Normal male group.
4. Prostitutes were significantly more extroverted and more neurotic than the Normal female group.

The present result supported the view of Eysenck (1963) that extroverted behaviour includes greater alcohol and cigarette consumption as well as high risk taking and more frequent alteration of behaviour. Stability-neuroticism, the second basic EPI dimension, may also be significantly related to the development of deviant drug and alcohol consumption patterns. The present result is also confirmed by the results of Higgins and Marlatt (1973), and Vogel (1961) who reported the alcoholics to be high on neuroticism. The findings of Allsopp and Feldman (1976) also confirm the present results. They found that children who had engaged in anti-social behaviour were higher in psychoticism, neuroticism and extroversion than well-behaved boys. The findings of Lorefice, Steer, Fine and Schut (1976) are also in favour of present results. Longitudinal studies (Kammeier *et al.*, 1973) usually show attributes such as impulsivity and hostility as predisposing to alcoholism rather than neuroticism, Orford (1976) reported that when alcoholics are successfully treated, their N scores are reduced to normal along with their drinking behaviour. So the reason behind the Alcoholics being extrovert and neurotic are that they may fit either into the dysthymic or the hysteric quadrants of the EPI, with the result that the overall correlation between E and alcoholism is largely cancelled (Eysenck, 1981). Early expectations that alcoholics would be extroverted were probably based on observations that behaviour becomes more extrovert when the individual is given alcohol. But than, it can be predicted from arousal theory that the person whose behaviour is already extroverted would have less need of alcohol. In the light of the above discussions the present finding stands confirmed.

Being a disorganized group beggars were significantly different on extroversion as well as neuroticism from the normal group. The results showed them to be introvert and stable. The reason seems to be their realisation that they have very little social prestige and position in society. In case of most of the beggars, it was seen that poverty and unguided childhood were the two most striking factors that stood out prominently. It implies that home should have sufficient means to maintain the minimum standards of living so as to meet physical and emotional needs of the growing child. The child develops the sense of belonging through love and care of his parents and other family members. Lack of love and continued neglect do not develop self-confidence in themselves and suppressed all wishes of their life. Also they develop a sense of insecurity, inferiority etc. which give birth to introvert personality trait. Thus they represent an immature personality. They are emotionally naive and labour under the delusion that their own subjective states must necessarily infect others. Thus, due to their pitiable condition, they can't revolt against the society, and under these circumstances they develop introvert and stable personality (Jha, 1987). Thus, the present findings are confirmed.

Eysenck (1958) has found the recidivist prisoners to be significantly more neurotic than the normals, but the two groups could not be differentiated on the extroversion-introversion dimension. Singh (1981) used PEN Inventory to find out the extroversion-neuroticism and psychoticism in criminals and found that criminals scored significantly higher on P and N. Studies conducted on Indian sample (Agrawal, 1961; Hoch, 1962; Luthra, 1957 and Shanmugham and Sundari, 1962) have also confirmed the presence of more neuroticism in criminals. Singh (1981) and Ranga (1982) also found that criminal group scored significantly high on extroversion and neuroticism. In the present study it is found that criminals scored significantly high on extroversion as well as on neuroticism. Therefore, the results supported the contension that criminal fall in the psychopathic quadrant. The bulk of evidence does support the revised 'three factor' theory of the personality predisposition to criminality, although of the three, E is the least strongly and reliably implicated (Eysenck and Eysenck, 1971; Wilson and MacLean, 1974; Eysenck and Eysenck, 1977; Eysenck, 1977). A more detailed analysis of the particular items which differentiate criminals from non-criminals confirms the suspicion that in so far as E is associated with criminality, it is the impulsivity aspect, rather than sociability, which is responsible for this connection (Eysenck and Eysenck, 1971).

The findings that criminals are higher on neuroticism can be explained on the fact that N is a measure of emotional instability. The individuals who are emotionally unstable are likely to have little control over their emotions, feelings and impulses. The criminals, being high on emotionality, have as such weak control over their emotions, feelings and impulses. Thus, they are more susceptible to antisocial activities at slightest provocation. The conclusion that criminals would be higher on

N has been drawn consistently by a large number of studies (i.e. mentioned above). On the other hand sociability is one of the constituent part of the E factor, but it may be less in any case, the above results support the idea that criminals in general, can be differentiated on the basis of personality scores. To what extent these personality scores are influenced by the criminal's environmental situation, for example, the fact that very often they are tested after incarceration is an open question, but there is little doubt that some biological factors are involved.

Glover (1953) and Greenwald (1970) point out the secondary role of the economic motive in prostitution and assert that the environmental factors that lead to prostitution are essentially psychological. They emphasize that psychological or emotional environment in early and later childhood are responsible for it, arguing that in the last analysis even economic hardship is a form of psychological stress, which more than anything else precipitates socially deviant conduct including the sexually deviant act of prostitution (Glover, 1953). Psychoanalysts like Adler (1932) have propagated the theory that prostitution depends on personality and that it is the defect, maladjustment or pathological condition in the personality which causes a woman to prostitute herself. According to him it is the psychic make up of certain men and women that calls for prostitution. Glover (1953) emphasises that the choice prostitution as a profession is determined by the early history of infantile sexual impulse and that the problem cannot be measured without a collateral investigation of the sexual development of the male. In fact, Greenwald (1969) hypothesized that lack of close parental ties coupled with early rewarded sexual experience made these girls vulnerable to prostitution.

The psychologists and psychoanalysts like Agoston (1945), Glover (1953), Caprio (1954) and Greenwald (1958) who have studied prostitutes including call girls, emphasize that fact of adequate family love, understanding, care and attention in early and later childhood whether caused by the immediate economic or emotional problems facing the mother or parents or by their being emotionally inadequate, maladjusted or immature people incapable of imparting the required love—is the unmistakable environmental or psychological factor contributing to prostitution. And due to which Glover (1945) appropriately remarked that the prostitute—to be has a neurotic personality and it is her psychological set up or personality which makes her accepts the suggestion to be a prostitute or call girl. Rolph (1955) while agreeing with it stresses that the important aspect of personality with regard to causation is 'character disorder' which itself is the result of the processes causing social maladjustment. It appears that it is the defect in the formation of the ego rather than of the superego that are responsible for prostitutions (Rolph, 1955). Eysenck (1976) reported on a series of studies concerned with connections between personality and sexual attitude and behaviour. A questionnaire was constructed containing over 100 items. The attitude items were factor analysed to reveal 14 factors at the primary level. These 14 factors were collapsed into two broader 'super factors', which were called libido and satisfaction. When the two main factors were correlated with personality, it was found that libido was associated with High P and to a lesser extent high E and N. Satisfaction was most strongly linked with N and to a lesser extent with P and E. High E subjects are particularly high on promiscuity and low on nervousness and prudishness. High N scores are high on excitement, nervousness, hostility, guilt and inhibition factors and low on satisfaction. High P scores are high on curiosity, premarital sex, promiscuity and hostility.

Analysis of self-reported sexual behaviour in relation to personality (Eysenck, 1981) revealed that high E subjects have the characteristics of a prostitute. High N and high P scores both show a "pathological or 'non-conorming' pattern of sexual reactions. Both report strong sex drives, but whereas high Ps tend to act out their libidinous, promiscuous and oral desires, high Ns do not. It seems that the inhibitions, worries and guilt feelings of neurotics prevent them from consummating their desires. Both high Ns and high Ps report dissatisfaction, but for different reasons, neurotics because they are repressed and psychotics because they are insatiable. Since it has often been supposed that sexual deviates are lacking in the social skills necessary for normal sexual contact, items referring to shyness and social difficulty were specifically examined (Gosselin & Wilson, 19>80). It appears that the sadomasochists, transvestites and transsexuals are particularly shy and sensitive, while the leather fetishists and dominant women deny such tendencies. All the deviant groups are, however, susceptible to loneliness and depression. According to Eysenck (1981) these people take life and themselves quite seriously, all of the deviant groups were significantly less likely to enjoy telling jokes to their friends.

Results of the present study showing the prostitutes to have higher score on both the dimensions, i.e. on E and N as compared to the normals can be explained on the lines of arguments above.

IV
Summary, Limitations and Suggestions

The present research was undertaken to examine the differences between organized and disorganized (Alcoholics, Beggars, Criminals and Prostitutes) subjects on personality factors, such as Frustration, Anxiety, Hostility and Extroversion-Neuroticism. On the basis of review of the studies the following hypotheses were formulated and tested.

1. There will be significant difference in the mean regression-frustration score af disorganized groups (Alcoholics-A, Beggars-B, Criminals-C and Prostitutes-D) and normal persons.
2. There will be significant difference in the mean fixation-frustration score of disorganized groups (Alcoholics-A, Beggars-B, Criminals-C and Prostitutes-D) and normal persons.
3. There will be significant difference in the mean resignation-frustration score of disorganized groups (Alcoholics-A, Beggars-B, Criminals-C and Prostitutes-D) and normal persons.
4. There will be significant difference in the mean aggression-frustration score of disorganized groups (Alcoholics-A; Beggars-B, Criminals-C and Prostitutes-D) and normal persons.

5. There will be significant difference between the mean anxiety score of disorganized groups (Alcoholics-A, Beggars-B, Criminals-C and Prostitutes-D) and normal persons.
6. There will be significant difference between the mean hostility score of disorganized groups (Alcoholics-A, Beggars-B, Criminals-C and Prostitutes-D) and normal persons.
7. There will be significant difference between the mean extroversion score of disorganized groups (Alcoholics-A, Beggars-B, Criminals-C and Prostitutes-D) and normal persons.
8. There will be significant difference between the mean neuroticism score of disorganized groups (Alcoholics-A, Beggars-B, Criminals-C and Prostitutes-D) and normal persons

The study was conducted on a sample of 200 disorganized personalities consisting of 50 male Alcoholics (A), 50 male Beggars (B), 50 male Criminals (C) and 50 female Prostitutes (D). Also 100 normal male and 100 normal female subjects were taken as control group. The two groups were matched for their age, sex, religion and culture, size of the family, economic status etc. To examine the proposed differences between variables/test of mean differences were calculated. The following results were obtained as a result of the comparisons made on frustration, anxiety, hostility and extroversion-neuroticism scale.

Results showed that the Alcoholics and Criminals had significantly higher mean regression score as compared to the normal male group. The prostitutes had also higher mean regression score as compared to the normal female group, but the difference was not significant. The Alcoholic, Beggar, Criminal and Prostitute have been found to display more fixated behaviour as compared to their normal groups. It was also found that Beggars and Criminals display significantly less resignated response and aggressive response as compared to the normal sample. While no significant difference has been observed in the resignated response and aggressive response of Alcoholic and normal male sample, however, Prostitutes had significantly greater mean resignation score as compared to the normal female sample. No significant difference between the aggressive response of prostitutes and normal female sample was observed.

On the anxiety scale all the four samples (Alcoholics, Beggars, Criminals and Prostitutes) of experimental group had significantly high mean score than their control groups. Again experimental groups were distinguished from control groups on hostility test. And it was found that all the four groups of disorganized personalities (Alcoholics, Beggars, Criminals and Prostitutes) were significantly high on hostility. Therefore, it was concluded that experimental groups (Alcoholics, Beggars, Criminals and Prostitutes) were more anxious and more hostile than their normal samples. Further the four groups of disorganized personalities (Alcoholics, Beggars, Criminals and Prostitutes) were distinguished from normals on extroversion and neuroticism, and the results were that Alcoholic? were significantly high on extroversion as well on neuroticism, Beggars were significantly low on both the dimensions, i.e. extroversion-neuroticism. Lastly, Criminals and Prostitutes were significantly high on extroversion and neuroticism.

Limitations and Suggestions

The present study, like many others in the field of social disorganization is not free from certain limitations. The etiology and personality of socially disorganized individual is so complex and interwoven that a study like the present one cannot claim to present a comprehensive analysis and causation of problems of society entirely.

Firstly, the study does not pretend to present a complete picture of the personality of disorganized groups. Only a few personality factors were taken into account and no claim can be made of describing the disorganized personality in its entirety.

A more thorough study including many other relevant personality factors (Self-concept, self-disclosure, rigidity, adjustment, authoritarianism, achievement motivation etc.) and using projective techniques and depth analysis would be able to demonstrate personality difference between the organized and disorganized groups in a comprehensive way.

Secondly, parental discipline seems to be the one important variable influencing many personality dimensions. Its role in causing disorganisation needs attention of the researchers.

Thirdly, child-rearing practices are also very important variable which influence the personality and therefore, merit study.

Fourthly, the disorganized personalities not only differ with the normal persons but they differ among themselves in terms of their personality dimension. But there is dearth of studies showing personality differences among the different disorganized groups.

It must be confessed that the present investigation is limited in scope because it is a field study leaning mainly on questionnaire and interview method. And it is very difficult to interview or administer questionnaire to such varied groups like prostitutes and beggars, criminals and alcoholics. Therefore, it is necessary to conduct studies employing clinical method and observation method to gain more insight into sensitive areas such as identity crisis and interpersonal conflicts. Also studies need to be undertaken to justify the appropriate role of personality dimensions of socially disorganized individuals.

References

Abraham, K. (1953) *Selected Papers on Psychoanlaysis*, New York: Basic Books Inc.

Adler, A. (1932) *Individual-Psychology*. London: Routledge and Kegan Paul.

Agoston, T. (1945) "Psychological Aspects of Prostitution—The Pseuao Personality". *International J. of Psycho-analysis*, London.

Agrawal, K.G. (1961) "Study of neuroticism among the convicts of a person." *J. Correct.* W. K., 8, 78-83.

Akhtar, S.N. (1970) "Attitude modifiability as a function of some personality factors." Unpublished Ph.D. Thesis, Bhagalpur University.

Allardt, E. (1957) "Drinking Norms and Drinking Habits," in *Drinking and Drinkers*. Helsinki: Finnish Foundation for Alcohol Studies.

Allsopp, J.F. and Feldman, M.P. (1976) "Personality and anti-social behaviour in school boys." *Br. J. Criminal.* 16, 337-351.

Arudu, (1893) "Aleune anomalienella prostitute", Turin.

Argyle, M. (1964) *Psychology and Social Problems*. London: Methuen.

Barker, R.; Dembo, T. and Lewin, K. (1941) "Frustration and Regression: An experiment with young children." Studies in Topological and Vector Psychology, 11 Univ. la. stud, child welf., 18, 1,314.

Baugh, V.S. and Carpenter, B.L. (1962) "A comparison of

delinquents and non-delinquents." *J. Soc. Psychol.*, Vol. 56, 73-78.

Bengal Vagrancy Act (VII of 1943) *In Social Problems and Social Disorganization in India*, Memoria, C.B. 1970. Kitab Mahal.

Berkowitz, L. (1962) *Aggression: A Psychological Analysis*. New York: McGrow Hill Book Company.

Biel, W.C., and C. Kelly (1942) "The Effect of Cortical Lessons on Emotional and Regression behaviour in the rat: II Regression Behaviour." *J. Comp. Psychol.*, 30 241-254.

Bihar Prevention of Beggary Act (I of 1952) *Social Problems and Social Disorganization in India*. Memoria, C.B. 1970. Kitab Mahal.

Blackburn; R. (1968) "Personality in relation to extreme aggression in Psychiatric offenders." *Brit. J. Psychiat*, Vol. 11-4, 821-828.

Black Stone, W. (1972) *Commentaries on the Laws of England*.

Bombay Beggars Act (XXIII of 1945) *Social Problems and Social Disorganization in India*. Memoria. C.B. 1970, Kitab Mahal.

Burner, J.S. and Goodman, C.C. (1947) "Value and need as organizing factors in Perception". *J. Abnorm Social Psychol.*, Vol. 43, 33-44.

Buikhnisen, W. (1982) "Aggressive behaviour and Cognitive disorders." *Internal Journal of Law and Psychiatry*. Vol. 5 (2), 205-217.

Burgess, P.K. (1972) "Eysenck's theory of Criminality: A new approach." *Brit. J. of Crime*, Vol. 12, 74-82 (a).

Burgess, P.K. (1972). "Eysenck's theory of Criminality: A test of some objections to disconfirmatory evidence." *Brit. J. of Soc. and Clin. Psychology*, Vol. II, 248-256 (b).

Burnstein, E. and Worchel, P. (1962) "Arbitrariness of frustration and its consequences for aggression in a social situation." *J. of Personality*, 30, 528-540.

Buss, A.H. (1961) *The Psychology of Aggression*. New York: Wiley.

Buss, A.H. (1971) "Aggression Pays". In J.L. of Singer (Ed.) *The control of aggression and violence: Cognitive and Psychological factors.* New York: Academic Press.

Buss, A.H. and Durkee, A. (1957) "An inventory for aggressing different kinds of hostility." *J. Consult. Psycho.*, 21, 343-348.

Cameron, N.A. (1947) *The Psychology of Behaviour Disorders: A Bio-social Approach.*

Caprio, F.S. (1954) *Female Homosex vality*, New York: The Citadel Press.

Cattel, R. (1957) *Personality and Motivation: Structure and Measurement.* New York: World Book Company.

Chandra, S. (1967) *Prostitution in Sociology of Deviation in India*, Bombay: Allied Publishers

Chauhan, N.S. and Tiwary, G.P. (1972) *Guide to using Nairashya Maapa*, Agra Psychological Research Cell.

Chesser, E. (1958) *Live and Let live.* London: William Heinemann Ltd.

Chesser, E. (1971) *Strange Loves.* New York: Popular Library edition, William Morrow and Company Inc.

Child, I.L. (1946) "Children's Preference for goals, easy or difficult to obtain." *Psychol. Monogr.*

Choisy, M. (I960) *A Month Among the Girls.* New York: Pyramid.

Cleckley, H. (1948) *The Psychopath, a Problem for Society*. Federal Probation, 12, 3-8.

Clinard, M.B. (1963) *Sociology of Deviant Behaviour.* New York: Chicago-San Francisco.

Clominger, C.R., Christansen, K.O., Reich, I. and Gottesman, I.I. (1978) "Implications of sex differences in the prevalances of anti-social personality, alcoholism and criminality for familial transmission." *Arch. of Gen. Psytry.*, Vol. 35 (8), 941-951.

Cohen, A.K. (1955) *Delinquents boys: The culture of the gang*. Glencoe, Illinois: Free Press.

Cole, K.E.; Fisher, G. and Cole, S.S. (1968) "Women who kill: A Socio-Psychological study" *Arch. Gen. Psychiat.* Vol. 19, 1-8.

Cowen, E.L.; Zax, M.; Klein, R.; Izzo, L.D. and Trost, M.A. (1965) "The relation of anxiety in school children to school record, achievement and behaviour measures." *Child Development*, 36, 685-695.

Cooley, C.H. (1909) *Social organization: A study of the large mind*. New York: Charles Seribuer's Sons.

Davis, K. (1971) "Sexual Behaviour (Prostitution), in contemporary social problems". ed. by Robert K. Marton and Robert A. , New York: Nisbet.

Davis, M.S. (1971) "That's interesting", *Philosophy of the Social Sciences*. 1, 309-344.

Devi, G.B-(1969) "A study of anxiety in men and women college students." *Psychol. Stud.*, 14, 35-38.

Diamond, S. (1934) "Habit Formation under Non-selective conditions." *J. Comp. Psychol.*, 17, 109-122.

Dillnbergerova, Y. (1969) (Eysenck's EPI answer sheet) Psychologia, Zboruik Filozofickej Fukulty University Komensheko, 20, 141-145.

Dollard, J. (1937) "Drinking Mores of the Social classes." *Alcoholic Science and Society*, 99.

Dollard, J.; Doob, L.W.; Miller, J.E.; Mowrer, O.H. and Sears, R.R. (1939) *Frustration and Aggression*. London: Yale University Press. New Haven.

Dollard, J. *et al.* (1944) *Frustration and Aggression*, London: Yale University Press, New Haven.

Dorcus, R.M. and Shafer, G.W. (1945) *Text book of Abnormal Psychology*. 3rd. ed., Baltimore: Williams and Wilkins Company.

Durkheim, E. (950) *The rules of sociological method*. Glencoe. Illinois: The Free Press.

Dutt, N.K. (1968) "A study of relationship of anxiety with age and professional hierarchy." *J. Psychol. Res.*, 12, 33-36.

Dutt, N.K (1964) "Psychological and educational implications of the concept of mental health in Indian thought." Unpublished Ph.D. Thesis. Panjab University, Chandigarh.

Edwards, G., Kyle, E., and Nicholls, P. (1977) "Alcoholics admitted to four hospitals in England: III Criminal records." *Journal of Studies on Alcohol*. Vol. 38 (9), 1648-1664.

Elliot, D.S. (1974) *Diversion—A study of Alternative Processing Practices*. Washington D.C., Department of Health, Education and Welfare.

Elliot, H.M. (1932) "Relationship of Drive to Learning." *Psychol. Bull.*, 29, 644.

Elliot, M.A. and Merill, F.E (1950) *Social Disorganization* (3rd Edit.) New York: Harper and Brothers Publishers.

Esselslyn, T.C. (196S) "Prostitution in the United States." Annals of American Academy of Political and Social Sciences, 376.

Eysenck, H.J. (1958a) *Manual of Maudsley Personality-Inventory*, London: University Press.

Eysenck, H.J. (1958b) "A short Questionnaire for the measurement of two dimensions of personality." *J. Appl. Psy.*, 42, 14-17.

Eysenck, H.J. (1962) "Response set, authoritarianism and personality Questionnaires." *Brit. J. Soci. Clin. Psychol.*, 1, 20-24.

Eysenck, H.J. (1963) "Biological basis of personality." *Nature*, 199, 1031-1034.

Eysenck, H.J. (1964) *Crime and Personality*. London: Paladin Books.

Eysenck, H.J. (1976) "Sex and Personality." London: Open Books.

Eysenck, H.J. (1977) "Crime and Personality" 2nd edn. London: Routledge & Kegan Paul.

Eysenck, H.J. (ed.) (1981) *A model for personality*. Springer-Verlag, Berlin, Heidelberg, New York.

Eysenck, H.J. and Eysenck, S.B.G. (1964) *Manual of the Eysenck Personality Inventory*. London: London University Press.

Eysenck, H.J. and Eysenck, S.B.G. (1977) *Manual for the EPI (French edn.)* London: Centre for Applied Psychology.

Eysenck, S.B.G. and Eysenck. H.J. (1963a) "The Validity of Questionnaires and rating assessments of extroversion and neuroticism and their factorial stability." *Brit. J. Psychol.*, 54, 51-62.

Eysenck, S.B.G. and Eysenck, H.J. (1969) "Scores on three personality variables as a function of age, sex and social class." *Br. J. Soc. Clin. Psychol.*, 8, 69-76.

Eysenck, S.B.G. and Eysenck, H.J. (1970) "Crime and Personality: An empirical study of the three-factor theory." *Br. J. Criminal*, 10, 225-239.

Faretra, G. (1981) "A profile of aggression from adolescence to adulthood: A 18-year follow of psychiatrically disturbed and violent adolescent." *American J. of Orthopsychiatry*, Vol. 51 (3), 439-453.

Faris, R.E.L. (1948) "Contemporary and Perspective Social Disorganization." *Sociology and Social Researches*, No. 32.

Fowler, R.C., Liskow, B.I., and Tanna, V.L. (1980) "Alcoholism depression and life events." *J. of affective disorders*, Vol. 2 (2), 127-135.

French, L. and Byce, F.O. (1978) "Suicide and female aggression: A contemporary analysis of anomic suicide." *J. of Clin. Psytry.*, Vol. 39 (10), 761-765.

Freud, S. (1933) *New Introductory Lectures on Psychoanalysis*. New York: Norton.

Frodi, A. (1978) "Experimental and Psychological responses associated with anger and aggression in women and men." *J. of Research in Personality*, Vol. 12 (3), 335-349.

Fuller, R.C. (1937) "Sociological theory and Social Problems." *Social Forces*, Vol. 15 (4), 496-502.

Giannell, A.S. (1966a) "Psychological need characteristics of Criminal offender groups." *J. Soc. Psychol.*, Vol. 69, 55-72.

Giannell, A.S. (1970) "The role of internal inhibition in crime causation. *J. Soc. Psychol.*, 81, 31-36.

Gillin, J.L. (1946) *The Wisconsin Prisoner.* Madison: The University of Wisconsin Press.

Gilpin, B.C. and Maltz, P. (1980) "The oppositional personality in childhood." *Child Psychiatry and Human Development*, Vol. 11 (2), 79-86.

Glover, E. (1945) *The Psychopathology of Prostitution London*, Revised, 1969, Institute for the Study of Delinquency.

Glover, E. (1953) *The Abnormality of Prostitution Women*, (ed.) AM. Krich, New York: Dell Publishing Company Inc.

Glueck, S. and Glueck, E. (1952) *Delinquents in the making*, New York: Harper and Row, 89.

Glueck, S. and Glueck, E. (1955) *Physique and delinquency*. New York: Harper and Row.

Glueck, S. and Glueck, E. (1960) *Unrevelling juvenile delinquency*. New York: Commonwealth Fund.

Gnapp, E.H.A. (1976) "Causal theory of alcoholism and drug addiction," *Psy.*, Vol. 13 (2), 3-23.

Gosselin, C. and Wilson, G.D. (1980) *Sexual Variations. Fetishism sadomasochism and transvestism*, London: Faber and Faber.

Gray, D. (1973) "Turning-out: A study of Teen age Prostitution." *Urban life and culture*, 1, 401-425.

Greenwald, H. (1958) *The Call-Girl—A Social and Psychoanalytical study*, New York: Ballentyne Books, Inc.

Greenwald, H. (1970) *The Elegant Prostitute—A social and Psychoanalytical study*. New York: Ballentyne Books, Inc.

Gulevich, G.D. and Bourne, P.G. (1970) "Mental illness and violence". In D.N. Daniels, M.F. Gilula, and F.M. Qchberg (Eds.) *Violence and the Struggle for existence*. Boston: Little, Brown.

Guze, S.B.; Tuason, V.B.; Gatfield, P.D.; Steward, M.A. and Picken, B. (1962) "Psychiatric illness and crime with particular reference to alcoholism: A study of 223 criminals." *J. of Nervous and Mental Disease*, 134, 512-521.

Haggard, H.W. (1945) "The effects of large and small amounts of alcohol." *Alcohol Science and Society*.

Hamilton, J.A. and Ellis, W.D. (1933) "Behaviour Constancy in Rat," *J. Genel. Psychol.*, 42, 120-153.

Harrison, G. (1948) "A sociological theory of psychopathy." *Amer. J. Socio.*, 53.

Hentic, H.V. (1947) *Crime, Causes and Conditions.* New York: McGraw Hill.

Higgins, R.L. and Marlatt, G.A. (1973) "The effects of anxiety arousal upon the consumption of alcohol by alcoholics and social drinkers." *J. Consult, and Clin. Psychol.*, 41, 426-433.

Hindman, M. (1977) "Child abuse and neglect the alcohol connection." *Alcohol Health and Research World,* Vol. 1, (3), 27.

Hoch, E.H. (1962) "Delinquent features in children examined at a private psychiatric centre." *J. Correct.* W.K., 9, 59-96.

Horney, K. (1945) *Our Inner Conflicts.* New York: W.W. Norton & Company.

Horrocks, J.E. (1964) *From Foreward to Crime and Personality,* first edition. London: Routledge and Kegan Paul.

Hundal, P.S. (1968) "Factorial structure of Psychometric measures of achievement motivation and their factorial structure." *Ind. J. Psychol.*, 47, 15-27.

Iwawaki, S.; Sujiyama, Y. and Nanri, R. (1964) *Japaneese manual of the Maudsley Personality Inventory,* Kyoto: Kyoto University Press.

Jackman, N.R.R.; O'Toole and Gilbert, G. (1967) "The self-image of the prostitutes" in J.H. Gagnon and W. Simon (eds.) *Sexual Deviance.* New York: Harper & Row.

Jackson, M.M. (1941) "Reaction tendencies of the White Rats in running and Jumping situations." J. *Comp. Psychol.*, 31, 255-262.

Jamuar, K.K. and Mishra, V.D. (1981) "A comparative study of some personality traits of first offenders and non-criminal," *Social Defence,* Vol. 77 (66), 19-22.

Jawa, M.S. (1973) "Birth order and age related changes in anxiety among adolescents." *Ind. J. Appl. Psychol.*, 10, 6-11.

Jessor, R. and Jessor, S.L. (1977) *Problem Behaviour and Psychosocial Development: A longitudinal study of youth.* New York: Academic.

Jha, M. (1979) *The Beggars of a Pilgrims City.* Nand Kishore Dwivedi, Varanasi.

Jha, J. P. (1987) Beggars-Social Parasites. *The Hindustan Times,* February 5.

Kafiluddin, S. (1977) "A study of paramental discipline, family, structure and oridenal position as antecedent factors in the genesis of aggression." Unpublished Ph.D. Thesis, Bhagalpur University.

Kammeier, M.L., Hoffmann, H., Loper, R.G. (1973) "Personality characteristics of alcoholics as college freshman and at time of treatment." *Qtly. J. Stud. Alcohol.*, 34, 390-399.

Kanekar, S. and Mukerjee, S. (1972) "Intelligence, extroversion and neuroticism in relation to reason of birth." *J. Soc. Psychol.*, 86, 309-310.

Kapur, P. (1978) *The life and world of call girls in India: A socio-psychological study of the Aristocratic Prostitutes.*" New Delhi: Vikas Publishing House Pvt. Ltd.

Keller, M. (1960) "Definition of Alcoholism." *Qtly. J. of Studies on Alcohol*, 21, 125-134.

Keller, M. (1977) "Alcoholism: Nature and Extent of the Problem." The Annals, 1958 in Mohan, B., *India's Social Problems*, Indian International Publication.

Kempt, T. (1970) "Physical and Psychological causes of Prostitution and the means of combating them," cited by Kapur, P. (1978) *The life and World of Call-Girls in India*. New Delhi: Vikas Publishing House, Pvt. Ltd.

Kishore, G.R. and Pandey, N.K. (1980) "Sex, anxiety and Intolerance of ambiguity," *Asian J. of Psych. and Edu.*, Vol. 6 (3), 1-3.

Kleemeirer, R.W. (1942) "Fixation and Regression in the Rat." *Psychol. Monogr.* 54 (4).

Kluckohn, C. and Kelly, W.H. (1945) "The concept of culture". in Rolph Linton, ed. *The science of Man in the World crisis*. New York: Columbia University Press.

Knap, R.R. (1962) "*Manual of the Maudsley Personality Inventory.*" California: Educational and Industrial Testing Science.

Kramer, R. (1943) "The Conceptional Status of Social Disorganization." *Amer. J. of Socio.*, No. 48, 467-476.

Krech, D.; Crutchfield, R.C. and Ballachey, E.L. (1962) *Individual in society*. McGraw Hill Inc.

Kregarmen, J.J. and Woichel, P. (1961) "Arbitrariness of frustration and aggression. *J. of Abnorm. and Soc. Psychol*, 63, 183-187.

Kretschmer, E. (1925) "Physique and Character". London: Routledge & Kegal Paul.

Krishna, K.P. (1971) "Manifest anxiety as a function of sex and education." *Behaviourmetic*, 1, 55-57.

Kumarappa, J.M. Ed. (1945) "Our Beggar Problem". Bombay: Padma Publications Ltd.

Kumari, P. (1957) *Alcohol Sales Experiment in Rural Finland*. Helsinki: Finnish Foundation for Alcohol Studies.

Kundu, S. and Mukherjee, K. (1958) "Social behaviour of Prisoners". *Indn. J. of Psychol.*, Vol. 33, 269-273.

Lai, J.N. (1969) "Sex differences in children's Personality." *Indn. Psychol. Rev.*, 5, 113-116.

Lall, S. (1970) "Who is a prostitute ?" *Social Health*, 8, 5.

Landis, B.Y. (1945) "Some Economic Aspects of Alcohol Problems." Memories of the Section on Alcohol and Studies. *Qtly. J. of Studies on Alcohol*, 28-29.

Lansky, L.M., Crandall, V.J., Kagan, J. and Baker, C.R. (1961) "Sex-differences in aggression and its correlates in Middle Class Adolescents." *Child. Dev.*, 32, 45-58.

Lapiere, R.T. & Franswortb, P.R. (1949) *Social Psychology*. New York: McGraw Hill.

Laufer, W.S. (1980) "Vocational interests of criminal offenders: A topological and demographic investigation." *Psychological Reports*, Vol. 46 (1).

Lawson, R. (1966) *Frustration, the Development of Scientific concept.*

Lemert, E.M. (1951) *Social Pathology: A Systematic approach to the theory of sociopathic behaviour*. New York: McGraw Hill, Book Co. Inc.

Lindquist, C.U., Lindsay, J.S. and White, G.D. (1979) "Assessment of assertiveness in drug abusers." *J. of Clin. Psych.*, Vol. 35 (3), 676-579.

Lombroso, C. (1911) *Crime, its causes and remedies*. Boston: Little Brown & Co.

Lorefiece, L.; Steer, R.A.; Fine, E.W. and Schut, J. (1976) "Personality traits and moods of alcoholics and heroin addicts." *J. of Studies on Alcohol.*, Vol. 37 (5), 687-689.

Luthra, B.R. (1957) "A study of some convicts in the central prison, Naini." *Siksha*, 9, 117-129.

Lynch, D. J. and Arnd, C. (1973) "Developmental changes in response to frustration among physically handicapped children." *J. of Personality Assessment*, Vol. 37 (2) 130-135.

Maier, N.R.F. (1940) "The Behaviour Mechanisms concerned with problem-solving", *Psychol. Rev.*, 47 43-58.

Maier, N.R.F. (1949) *Frustration. The Study of behaviour Without a Goal*. University of Michigan. New York, Toronto, London: McGraw Hill Inc.

Maier, N.R.F. and Klee, L.B. (1941) "Studies of abnormal behaviour in rat. VII, the permanent nature of abnormal fixations and their relation to convulsive tendencies." *J. Exp. Psychol.*, 29, 310-389.

Maier, N.R.F. and Klee, J.B. (1943) "Studies of abnormal behaviour in rat: XII, The Pattern of Punishment and its relation to abnormal fixation." *J. Exp. Psychol*, 32, 377-398.

Maerov, A. (1965) "Prostitution: A survey and review of 20 cases." *Psychiatric Qtly.*, 39, 675-701.

Malaviya, D. (1977) *Reactions to Frustration*. Research Foundation, New Delhi.

Mallick, S.K. and McCandles, B.R. (1966) "A study of catharsis of aggression." *J. of Person. and Soc. Psychol.*, 4, 591-596.

Mamoria, C.B. (1970) *Social Problems and Social Disorganization in India*. Kitab Mahal, 15, Thorn Hill Road, Allahabad.

Marquis, D.P. (1643) "A study of frustration in New born Infants." *J. Exp. Psychol.*, 32, 123-138.

Martin, R.F. (1940) "Native traits and regression in rats." *J. Comp. Psychol.*, 30, 1-26.

McCarthy, R.G. and Douglass, E.M. (1959) *Alcohol and Social Responsibility*. New York: Thomas Y. Cowell.

McClleland, D.C. and Liberman, A.M. (1949) "The effects of need for achievement on recognition of need related words." *J. Pers.*, 18 236.

McCord, W. and McCord, J. (1964) *The Psychopath*. Princeton, N-J.: Von Nostrand.

McCord, W.; McCord. J. and Howard, A. (1961) "Familial correlates of aggression in non delinquent males children." *J. Abnorm. Soc. Psychol*, 62, 79-93.

Mckee, L.P. and Leader, F.B. (1955) "The relationship of socio-economic status and aggression to the competitive behaviour of pre-school children". *Child Develop*.

McNamee, H.B.; Mello, N.K. and Mendelson, J.H. (1968) "Experimental analysis of drinking patterns of alcoholics: concurrent psychiatric observations." *Amer. J. of Psychiat.*, 124, 1063-1069.

McQuaid, J. (1970) "A personality profile of delinquents boy in Scottish approved schools". *Brit. J. Criminal*, 10, 147-157.

Mendelson, J.H.; LaDon. J. and Solomon, P. (1964) "Experimentally induced chronic intoxication and withdrawal in alcoholics: Psychiatric findings." *Qtly. J. of Studies on Alcohol*, Suppl. 2, 40-52.

Meyer. C.T. (1947) "The assertive behaviours of children as related to parent behaviour," *J. of Home Economics*, 39.

Miksik, O. (1978) "Structure of mental instability of the personality of a patient with psychogenic disorder of anxious-depressive nature." *Ceskoslovenska Psychologie*, Vol. 22 (1), 34-42.

Moore, D.R.; Chamberlain, P. and Mukal, L.H. (1979) "Children at risk of delinquency. A follow-up comparison of aggressive children and children who steal." *J. of Abnorm Child Psy.* Vol. 7 (3), 345-355.

Mowrer, E.R. (1942) "Disorganization-personal and social." Quoted by Memoria, C.B., 1970, *Social Problems and Social Disorganization in India*.

Mulvihill, D.J.; Tumin, M.M. and Curtis, L.A., Eds. (1969) *Crimes of violence* (Vol. 18). Washington, D.C.: U.S. Government Printing Office.

Murphy, G. (1947) *Personality: A Bio-social Approach to origins and structure*. New York & London.

Nagpur Survey (1961) *Social Problem and Social Disorganization in India*"– Memoria C.B. Allahabad: Kitab Mahal.

Ogburn, W.F. (1922) *Social change with respect to culture and original nature*. New York: B.W. Huebsch.

O'Kelly, L.I. (1940) "An Experimental Study of Regression. I. The behavioural characteristics of the regressive response." *J. Comp. Psychol*, 30, 41-53.

Orford, J. (1976) "A study of the personalities of excessive drinkers and their wives, using the approaches of Leary and Eysenck" *J. Consult. Clin. Psychol*, 44, 534-545.

Pareek, U.N. (1964) *Developmental Patterns in Reactions to Frustration*. New York: Asia Pub. House.

Parsons, T. (1951) *The social system*. New York: Free Press.

Parsons, T. and Kroeber, L. (1958) The concept of culture and of social system. *Ameri. Soc. Rev.*, 2, 502-583.

Pastore, N. (1952) "The role of arbitrariness in the frustration-aggression hypothesis." *J. of Abnorm. Soc. Psychol*, 41, 728-73.

Patjas, E. (1968) "Anxiety associated with school attendence and the grammer school entrance examination." *Res. Bull.*, 20, 16.

Patrick, C.H. (1952) *Alcohol, culture and society*. Durham, N.C.: Duke University Press. 12-39.

Pelka, S.M.D. and Slugocki, L. (1977) "Alcoholism and female Crime in Poland" *Int. J. of Offender Therapy and Comparative Criminology*, Vol. 21 (2), 174-183.

Peneston, E.G. (1978) "The Ego Strength Scale as a predictor of tte Indian suicide risk." *White Cloud. J.* Vol. 1 (2), 17-19.

Penny, R.K. (1965) "Reactive curiosity and manifest anxiety in children." *Child Dev.*, 36, 697-702.

Persons, R.W. (1970b) "Intermittent rein for cement, guilt and crime." *Psychol Rep.*, 26. 421-422.

Pestonjee, D.M. and Bagchi, R., (1979) "Anxiety and aggression. A study of Coronary Patients." *Indn. J. of Clin. Psy.*, Vol. 6 (1), 63-71.

Phillips. B.J.; Phillips, I.F. and Davidson, E.C. (1975) "Juvenile delinquent drug abuse in female: A clinical study." *Australian and New Zealand J. of Psychiat.*, Vol. 9 (4), 281-286.

Pingnier, F. (1972) "Phenomena of prostitution in the world of today." Rep. of the, 25th Int. Cong, of Int. Apolitionist Federation.

Pittman, D.J. and Gordon, C.W. (1958) *Revolving Door*. New York: The Free Press of Glencoe.

Poffenbenger, A.T. (1961) "Principles of Applied Psychology." Bombay: Allied Pacific.

Pramanick, M. (1980) "Child-rearing practices and Adult model personality." Unpublished Ph.D. Thesis, Bhagalpur University.

Prakash, J. and Tiwari, G.P. (1973) "Interest as a function of frustration type in dropout aetiology." *Manas*, Vol. 20 (1), 63-68.

Punekar, S.D. and Rao, K. (1962) *A Study of Prostitutes in Bombay*. Bombay: Lalvani Pub. House.

Punekar, S.D. and Rao, K. (1967) *A Study of Prostitutes in Bombay*." Bombay: Lalvani Pub. House.

Rangaswami, K. and Arunagiri, S. (1982) "Personality dimensions of criminal and mentally ill criminals." *Indn. J. of Psychiat*. Vol. 24 (1) 88-91.

Rao, S. and Singh, S. (1981) "Sex-type, income level and age in relation to reaction to frustrations: An Indian Slady." *Zeitschrift fur Psychologic*. Vol. 189 (2), 206-213.

Ratan, K. (1961) "Beggari Problem in Kanpur." *Indn.J. of Soc. Work*. Vol. 21 (4), 397-398.

Rauchfieisch, U. (1981) "Age and sex related changes in the reaction to frustration in children and adolescents." *Praxisder Kinder Psychologie and Kinder Psychiatric*, Vol. 30 (2), 55-62.

Riesman, D., Potter, J.R., and Watson, J. (1960) "The Vanishing Host." *Human Organization*, 19, 17-28.

Rizfo, N.D. (1982) "Murder in Boston. Killers and their Victims." *Int. J. of Offender and Comparative Criminology*, Vol. 26 (1), 36-42.

Robert, K.M. (1957) *Social theory and social structure*. (rev. edn.) New York: The Free Press of Glenoc.

Robinson, D. (1942) "Social Disorganization Reflected in Middle-class Drinking and Dancing Recreational Patterns." *Social Forces*, 20, 455-459.

Roe, A. (1945) "Children of Alcoholic Parents Raised in Foster Homes,"' *Alcohol Scien. and Society*, 124.

Rolph, C.H. (ed.) (1955) *Women of the streets*. London: Seeker and Warburg.

Rotbams, P. and Worchel, P. (1960) "The inhibition of aggression under non-arbitrary frustration." *J. of Personality*, 28, 108-117.

Ruch, F.L. (1958) *Psychology and Life*. Fifth Edition. Foreman and Co.

Saklofske, D.M. and Eysenck, S.B. (1980) "Personality and anti-social behaviour in delinquent and non-delinquent boys." *Psycho. Rep*. Vol. 47 (3), 1255-1261.

Saiason, G.I. and Spielberger, D.O. (1975) *Stress and Anxiety*, Vol. 2. Washington, DC: Hemisphere Pub. Corporations.

Satyarthi, M.K. (1977) "Anxious attitude of students in relation to some background variables." 64th session of Indn. Sc. Cong.

Schuessler, K.F., and Cressey, D.R. (1950) "Personality Characteristics of Criminals." *Amer. J. of Soc.* 5, 416-484.

Scott, H. (ed.) (1961) "Concise Encyclopaedia of Crime and Criminals." Quoted by Varma, P. Sahitya Bhavan, Agra.

Sears, R.R., Maccoby, E.E. and Levin, H. (1957) *Patterns of child-rearing*. Evanston, III Row, Peterson. New York: Harper & Row.

Seemannova, M. (1971) "A view of anxiety of children of 13 to 15 years of age." *Psychologia*, 22, 157-176.

Selznick, G.J. and Selznick, P. (1964) "A Normative Theory of Culture." *Amer. Soc. Rev*., 29, 653-669.

Shanmugam, T.E. and Sundari, T.A. (1962) "Difference between delinquent boys and non-delinquent boys in inhibition, disinhibition and Personality traits." *Psychol. Stud.*, 7.

Shaw, C.R., and Makay, H.D. (1931) "Social factors in juvenile delinquency." Rep. of National Commission on Law Observance and Enforcement, Part IV, Washington, D.C.

Sheldon, W.H. (1949) *Varieties of delinquent youth.* New York: Harper & Row.

Sheldon, W.H.; Strevens, S.S. and Tucker, W.B. (1940) *The Varieties of Human Physique*. New York: Harper.

Sherman, Cf. M. and Josh, H., (1942) "Frustration Reaction of normal and neurotic persons." *J. Psychol.*, 13, 3-19.

Silber, D.F. and Courtless T.F. (1968) "Measures of fantasy aggression among mentally retarted offenders." *Amer. J. Ment. Def.* Vol. 72, 918-923.

Sills, D.L. (ed.) (1968) *International Encyclopaedia of Social Sciences.* 12. New York: The Macmillan Co. and the Free Press.

Singh, A., (1978) "A study of personality traits." *Indn. J. of Clin. Psy.* Vol. 5 (2) 179-184.

Singh, A. (1981) "A study of Personality and Adjustment of Criminals." *Indian Psych. Rev.,* Vol. 20 (4), 31-38.

Singh, A.K. (1976) "Social disadvantage, intelligence and scholastic achievement." Paper presented at the 14th annual conference of Indn. Academy of App. Psych. IIT, Kharagpur, 27-29.

Singh, S.B. and Nigam, A. (1973) "A Comparative study of Personality Profile of the male and female medical students." *Indn. J Psychomet. Educ.*, 4, 30-33.

Singh, U.P. (1968) "Neuroticism and extraversion on an Indian Sample." *Ind. Psychol. Rev*. 5, 35-39.

Sinha, D. (1961b) "Anxiety and academic performance." *Psychologia,* 4, 119-122.

Sinha, D. (1963) "Manifest anxiety on an Indian Sample." *J. Gen. Psycho.*, 69, 261-265.

Sinha, D. (1965) "An analysis of anxiety areas and manifestations" a factorial study." *J. Psycho. Res.*, 9, 55-62.

Sinha, D. (1965a) "Validation of an anxiety scale". *J. Psycho. Res.*, 9, 19-26.

Sinha, D. (1968) "Manual for Sinha W-A Self-analysis from (anxiety Scale)." Rupa Psychological Corporation, Varanasi.

Sinha, J.K. (1975) "Anxiety in male and female adolescents." *Manas*, 22, 13-15.

Sollenberger, R.T. (1968) "Chinese-American Child-rearing practices and juvenile delinquency. *J. Soc. Psycho.* 74, 23-33.

Summer, W.G. and Keller, C. (1927) *The Science of Society*. New Haven. Conn.: Yale University Press.

Survey Report (1958) *Committee on Social and Moral Hygiene*, C.S.W.B., New Delhi.

Sutherland, E.H.; Schsoeder, H.C. and Tordella C.L. (1950) "Personality traits and the Alcoholic: A critique of Existing Studies." *Qtly. J. of Studies on Alcohol*, 11, 547-561.

Sutherland, E.H. and Donald, R.C. (1974) *Criminology*, Philadelphia: Lippincott.

Sulton, M.S. and Carlson, H.M. (1977) "Personality differences among men and women studing police science." *J. of Soc. Psycho.*, Vol. 102 (1), 161-162.

Svamum; Levitt, E.E. and McAdoo, W.G. (1982) "Differentiating male and female alcoholics from psychiatric out patients: The MacAndrew and Rosenberg alcoholism scales." *J. of Personality Assessment*. Vol. 46 (1), 81-84.

Synder, C.R. (1958) *Alcohol and the Jews*. New York: The Free Press of Glencoe.

Tappan, P.W. (1947) "Who is a Criminal ?" *Amer. Soc. Rev.*, Vol. 12 (1), 100.

Taylor, J.A. (1953) "Personality scale of manifest anxiety". *J. Abnorm. Soc. Psycho.*, 48, 285-290.

Taylor, S.P.; Schmutte, G.T. and Leonard, K.E. (1977) "Physical aggression as a function of alcohol and frustration." *Bull. of Psymic. Society.* Vol. 2 (3), 217-218.

Thomas, W.I. and Znaniecke, F. (1921) "The Polish peasent in Europe and America," New York:Alfred A. Knopf, Inc. Vol. 2, 1127-1131.

Thorne, F.C. and Pishkin, V.A. (1975) "A factorial study of needs in relation to life styles." *J. Clin. Psy.*, 31, 240-248.

Tucker, I.F. (1970) *Adjustment, models and mechanism*. New York: Academic Press.

Tylor, E. (1871) *Primitive Culture: Researches into the Development of Methodology, Philosophy, Religion, Language, Art and Custom*. London: J. Murray.

Tylor, K. and Duttie, J.M. (1980) "Normative aggression in non-athletic versus ice hockey playing Canadian boys." *Intn. J. of Sport Psych.*, Vol. 11 (4), 231-239.

Underwood, B.J. (1949) "Experimental psychology: An introduction Appleton Century Craft." New York Inc.

U.N. Committee (1959) "The suppression of the Traffic in persons and of the Exploitation of the prostitution of others," Document No E/C N 5/338, New York, U.N.

Vaugham, G. and Taylor, A.J. (1966) "Clinical anxiety and conformity." *Percept. Mot. Skills*, 22, 719-722.

Vidhu, M. (1968) "The relationship of neuroticism and extraversion to intelligence and educational achievement at different age levels." Unpublished Ph.D. Thesis, Psych. Panjab University.

Vogel, M.D. (1961) "GSR Conditioning and personality factor in alcoholics and normals." *J. Abnorm. Soc. Psycho*, 63, 417-421.

Washbush, W.C. (1963) "Interaction cues involved in perception of authority figures by delinquents and non-delin quents." *Calif. J. Educ. Res.*, Vol. 14, 74-78.

WHO Expert Committee (1958) "Social Problems and Social Disorganization in India", Memoria, C.B. 1970, Kitab Mahal.

Wilsen, G.D. and Maclean, A. (1974) "Personality, attitudes and humour preferences of prisoners and controls." *Psycho. Rep.* 34, 847-854.

Winscox, C.N. and Brainerd, J.E. (1950) "A comparison of the reaction of white and Nigroes to frustration as measured by Rosenzweig Picture-Frustration Test." *Amer Psyc'nat.* 5.

Willets, D.G. (1948) "What can we do about sex crime?" *Saturday Evening Post*, 221: 31, Dec. 11.

Wolfgang, M.E. and Strohm, R.B. (1956) "The relationship between alcohol and criminal homicide." *Qtly. J. of Studies on Alcohol*, 7, 411-425.

Wood, A.L. (1961) "A socio-cultural analysis of murder, suicide, and economic crime in ceylon." *Amer. J. Social Rev.*, 26, 744-753.

Wright, H.F. (1937) "The influence of barriers upon strength of motivation." *Centr. Psycho. Theory* I No. 3.

Zillmann, D., Bryant, J. Cantor, J.R. and Day, K.D. (1971) "Irrelevance of mitigating circumstances in retaliatory behaviour at high levels of excitation." *J. of Res. in Perso*, 9, 282-293.

Zillmann, D. and Cantor, J.R. (1976 b) "Effect of timing of information about mitigating circumstances on emotional responses to provocation and retaliatory behaviour." *J. of Exp. Soc. Psycho.*, 12, 38-53.

Zillmann, D. (1979) "Hostility and Aggression," New Jersey: Lawrence Erlbaum Associates, Inc. Hillsdale.

Zulliger, H. (1956) *Jugendliche Diebe.* (*Youth thieves*) Heilpadag. Werkble; Vol. 25, 152-156.

Index